PREPARING THE
Successful
Coach

PREPARING THE
Successful
Coach

Matt Garrett, BA, MA, PhD

Associate Professor of Physical Education and Sports Studies
Loras College

JONES AND BARTLETT PUBLISHERS

Sudbury, Massachusetts

BOSTON　　TORONTO　　LONDON　　SINGAPORE

World Headquarters
Jones and Bartlett Publishers
40 Tall Pine Drive
Sudbury, MA 01776
978-443-5000
info@jbpub.com
www.jbpub.com

Jones and Bartlett Publishers Canada
6339 Ormindale Way
Mississauga, Ontario L5V 1J2
Canada

Jones and Bartlett Publishers International
Barb House, Barb Mews
London W6 7PA
United Kingdom

Jones and Bartlett's books and products are available through most bookstores and online booksellers. To contact Jones and Bartlett Publishers directly, call 800-832-0034, fax 978-443-8000, or visit our website, www.jbpub.com.

> Substantial discounts on bulk quantities of Jones and Bartlett's publications are available to corporations, professional associations, and other qualified organizations. For details and specific discount information, contact the special sales department at Jones and Bartlett via the above contact information or send an email to specialsales@jbpub.com.

Production Credits
Acquisition Editor: Jacqueline Ann Geraci
Senior Production Editor: Julie Champagne Bolduc
Senior Production Editor: Susan Schultz
Associate Editor: Amy Flagg
Associate Editor: Patrice Andrews
Production Assistant: Jessica Steele Newfell
Marketing Manager: Wendy Thayer
Marketing Associate: Meagan Norlund
Manufacturing Buyer: Therese Connell
Interior Design: Anne Spencer
Cover Design: Kristin E. Ohlin
Photo Researcher: Lee Michelsen
Composition: NK Graphics
Printing and Binding: Courier Stoughton
Cover Printing: Courier Stoughton

Photo Credits
Cover Image: © O'Jay R. Barbee/ShutterStock, Inc.; Section 1 Opener © Michelle Donahue Hillison/ShutterStock, Inc.; Section 2 Opener © Tony L. Moore/ShutterStock, Inc.; Section 3 Opener © Adam Tinney/ShutterStock, Inc.; Section 4 Opener © Anson Hung/ShutterStock, Inc.; Section 5 Opener © Timkiv Vitaliy Ivanovich/ShutterStock, Inc.; Section 6 Opener © Suzanne Tucker/ShutterStock, Inc.; Section 7 & 8 Openers © Shawn Pecor/ShutterStock, Inc.

6048

Printed in the United States of America
11 10 09 08 07   10 9 8 7 6 5 4 3 2 1

Contents

Preface

Thank you for your interest in *Preparing the Successful Coach*! This book is for coaches of all levels, with particular attention paid to high school coaches.

Preparing the Successful Coach offers something different from other coaching books, by emphasizing the components of a coach's responsibilities that are not specific to game strategy or skill development. This text covers the myriad of responsibilities and challenges of the coaching profession that are not always considered, but are equally important in determining one's success as a coach.

Chapter Topics

Preparing the Successful Coach is divided into 38 chapters within seven separate sections and one additional chapter of practice test questions. The seven sections are entitled Coaching Philosophy, A Coach's Constituents, Developing the Team, Team Psychology, Team Physiology, The Coach as Administrator, and Coaching Issues.

The first section includes five chapters describing different components of a coach's philosophy. A successful coaching philosophy advances beyond game strategies and "X's and O's."

The first chapter is devoted to developing a sound coaching philosophy while simultaneously describing characteristics that distinguish good coaches from bad coaches. The second chapter reviews ethical situations that coaches encounter and assists coaches in developing a solid ethical base for their coaching philosophy. Additional chapters in this first section ask a coach to give serious consideration to how he or she balances coaching with teaching and/or other professional duties, with family and personal obligations, and with future aspirations and professional advancement.

A successful coach needs the skills to communicate and build relationships with several different groups of individuals. *Preparing the Successful Coach*'s second section examines these different groups. Chapter 6 investigates the coach's relationship with the athletic director, school administrators, and other head coaches within the athletic department. The next chapter reviews the relationship between the head coach and the assistant coaches, including the dual responsibilities of evaluating and supporting them.

Chapter 8 describes the often-maligned relationship between the coach and parents, and provides strategies for coaches to prevent and overcome any rifts. A chapter is devoted to the relationship the high school coach should have with the junior high school coach as well as local club or amateur coaches. The final chapter in this section describes the coach's relationship with other constituents, such as booster clubs, local business people, and the media.

The book's third section investigates several components of formulating a team and subsequently developing team chemistry. The first chapter in this section reviews the considerations of selecting the squad, including the balancing of talent, attitude, and potential. Chapter 12 describes the ideal coach–player relationship while simultaneously investigating how, when, and if captains should be selected.

Chapter 13 studies how coaches treat both star and third-string athletes. The subsequent chapter elaborates on the third-string athlete, specifically discussing how a coach should utilize the bench while also describing how a coach should determine the starting lineup. Chapters on the issues facing multiple-sport athletes and coaches, team goals, and team rules and consequences complete the third section.

The fourth section of *Preparing the Successful Coach* deals with team psychology and includes three chapters. Chapter 18 reviews the coach's role in motivating student-athletes, whereas Chapter 19 reviews the coach's role and different strategies to build student-athletes' confidence. The section's final chapter covers confrontation and offers suggestions and multiple scenarios in which coaches must deal with conflict.

The fifth section offers chapters concerning student-athletes' physiology. Chapter 21 deals with both the issue of deciding when an injured student-athlete should return to action and the coach's responsibility to work with members of the team's medical staff. The next chapter is concerned with student-athletes' body composition and also provides coaches with information to assist players who are pregnant.

Chapter 23 defines ergogenic aids and provides information on their use with specific attention paid to supplementation. The final chapter reviews the effects of alcohol, tobacco, and illicit drugs while also providing coaches with advice on how to best monitor their use among student-athletes.

The sixth section contains six chapters detailing a coach's multiple administrative tasks. A coach's administrative tasks will be different depending on the school's hierarchical structure, the athletic director or principal's wishes, the availability of support staff, and the coach's expertise. *Preparing the Successful Coach* identifies the more common administrative tasks, while realizing it is not an all-inclusive listing.

The first chapter in this section provides considerations to take into account when planning an effective practice session. Chapter 26 deals with the components of making a game schedule, and Chapter 27 elaborates on the issues surrounding overnight trips and travel.

The unit's final three chapters include the coach's role in the college recruiting process, compiling statistics, and a coach's game day and off-season duties. The high school coach may have a large or small role in the recruitment of his or her student-athletes, depending on several variables. A coach has multiple responsibilities, related and unrelated to his or her coaching assignment, on the day of the game, and once the season is completed.

The final section consists of eight chapters on various issues surrounding the coaching profession. Chapter 31 provides information on legal issues involved with coaching. The next two chapters further discuss student-athletes who violate the law and hazing.

How coaches must combat classism and racism are combined in Chapter 34, whereas issues involving religion comprise the subsequent chapter. Chapter 36 discusses the coach's role in ensuring a student-athlete's academic success. Chapter 37 combines issues related to the sexuality of both the student-athlete and the coach and the issues faced by those who coach the opposite gender. The book's final traditional chapter reviews the coach's role during the summer and investigates how valuable the summer has become in a sports program.

Chapter 39 provides sample test questions covering material from the previous chapters. These questions are often broad enough to include information from multiple chapters and can function either as written essay questions or be used for group discussion.

Chapter Format

Each of the first 38 chapters offers a similar format. Each chapter begins with a preview of the issues to be covered. This preview also outlines some of the highlights of the forthcoming chapter sections: the background information, discussion questions, scenarios, practice exercises, and references.

A section providing background information follows the preview. This includes highlights of a review of the literature and/or additional information related to the topic. This material is often presented in outline form.

The key elements of *Preparing the Successful Coach* follow the background information: discussion questions and scenarios. The discussion questions force coaches to contemplate how they would answer challenging issues relevant to the topic. These questions ask coaches to answer both in generalizations and to recall specific situations they have experienced. Readers are often asked to specify "Why or why not?" to a previous answer. This provides the opportunity to expand discussion and forces coaches to critically analyze their own and each other's thoughts.

Scenarios follow the discussion questions. These scenarios, written in paragraph form and often formulated from real-life occurrences, ask coaches how they would handle a particular situation. The ability to think critically is also encouraged in this section, and coaches are challenged not to alter the scenario for their convenience, but instead to make the tough decision.

Additionally, chapters offer practice exercises in which coaches are asked to more formally articulate a stance or a plan from the chapter. These articulations are to be completed in written form and then shared with a coaching colleague in order to allow a critique of each person's efforts.

Many chapters conclude by providing web page, journal, and book listings for readers to review for further research on the topic.

Preparing the Successful Coach is best read with coaching colleagues or other aspiring coaches. The opportunity to discuss the questions and scenarios with coaches who have different levels of experience is an invaluable way to learn from each other and challenge each other's thoughts and opinions.

Preparing the Successful Coach offers coaches, coaching educators, and other readers a wealth of practical scenarios that explore the many issues coaches encounter on and off the field. These issues parallel several of the coaching competencies defined by the National Association of Sport and Physical Education and the National Council of Accreditation for Coaching Education, including philosophy and ethics, safety and injury prevention, organization and administration, and teaching and communication. Please enjoy!

Acknowledgments

Thank you to the following individuals who made this project possible: B.J. Betz, Tim Calderwood, Dr. Sara Glover, Katy Henderson, Teresa Kehe, Rick Little, Megan Noud, Maria Prendergrast, Dr. Edward Zalisko, and my wife, Cheryl, and children, Joseph, Michael, and Rachel.

Coaching Philosophy

CHAPTER

Developing a Coaching Philosophy: What Makes a Good Coach?

A good coach should not be measured quantitatively by winning percentages, championships, the number of his or her players who are on the honor roll, or former players playing at the college level. A good coach should instead be measured by the impact he or she has on the student-athlete's lives, both during and after their years together. A coach may be best measured by his or her player's recollections several years later.

Good coaches have a sound coaching philosophy. This philosophy often stems from a coach's personal values (Lumpkin & Cuneen, 2001), should guide the multiple decisions a coach encounters, and shapes the program's direction. Components may include offensive and defensive strategies and how and which skills are taught. However, successful philosophies reach a deeper level. These philosophies may include how student-athletes are motivated, the emphasis placed on winning in relation to skill development and team satisfaction, team discipline, and professional interaction with multiple constituents.

This chapter provides information on a successful coach's qualities and the areas where coaches should be held accountable. Also discussed are the five steps to guide the development of a personal philosophy of sport and questions to ask when a coach formulates his or her philosophy. The chapter follows with discussion questions on the characteristics defining a good coach and on how good coaches carry themselves. Specific questions ask readers to describe whether a coach has to balance their responsibility of winning games with improving a student-athlete's performance. Sometimes altering a player's mechanics may improve a student-athlete's performance in the long term, but could hurt the team in the short-term.

The chapter concludes with four scenarios in which coaches are asked what both a good coach and bad coach would do in particular situations. These situations involve a player openly disrespecting the coach, an opponent's unprofessional behavior, and a student-athlete who has made a crucial mistake. A practice exercise provides guidelines for a coach to develop his or her own coaching philosophy.

This section introduces coaches to the literature on formulating their personal philosophy, something that should ultimately guide the decisions made throughout their coaching career. It also introduces the areas where coaches should be held responsible and the National Association of Sport and Physical Education's eight coaching competencies. The latter two demonstrate that there is more to the coaching profession than simply organizing practices and winning contests.

1. Areas where coaches should be held responsible:
   a. Injury prevention and care
   b. Acting as a role model on and away from the playing arena
   c. Student-athlete's psychological well-being in relation to sport
   d. Instruction of sport-appropriate skills and strategies
   e. Proper conditioning and nutrition
   f. Student-athlete's behavior patterns and sportsmanship
   g. Fiscal responsibility
   h. Ability to have positive interactions with multiple constituents
   i. Ability to organize several administrative tasks

2. Components of a coach's evaluation (Cardone, 2006; Roustio, 2002):
   a. Completion of specified duties
   b. Communication and relationship skills with staff, athletes, parents, and community
   c. Competitiveness of teams
   d. Demonstration of emotional stability while under pressure
   e. Image projected on behalf of the school district and community
   f. Coaching styles
   g. Leadership qualities
   h. Coaching performance and game management
   i. Handling of administrative duties

3. Characteristics of "a favorite coach" (Kessel, 2003):
   a. Knows student-athletes don't care how much he or she knows about the sport until they know how much he or she cares about them
   b. Builds players who will look to themselves for the answers
   c. Can balance fun with competitiveness
   d. Is consistent, so players do not have to worry "which coach" is there
   e. Understands the game
   f. Uses substitutes as tools for the team and not punishment of a student-athlete
   g. Is a great role model and not a critic
   h. Teaches life's lessons more than sport techniques
   i. Praises players for doing things right instead of nagging about the inevitable errors

4. Five steps to guide the development of a personal philosophy of sport:
   a. Determine what is valued and why.
   b. Be aware of the goals that are most valued.
   c. Know the established values of the sport.
   d. Determine which behaviors will characterize you.
   e. Be sure that your behaviors are consistent with your values.

5. Five questions to initiate a self-critical reflective process leading to a coaching philosophy (Lumpkin & Cuneen, 2001):
   a. What is the basis for my values?
      i. Who are my mentors and how have they guided me?
   b. Do I value the rules for sport?
   c. What do I value in sport?

    d. How do my values affect others?
       i. Do I treat opponents with respect?
    e. What values are exhibited by others in my sport?
6. Questions to ask when formulating a coaching philosophy (Hoch, 2003):
    a. Is your approach educationally sound?
    b. Is your approach appropriate for your players?
    c. Is your philosophy ethical?
    d. Will your approach last over the years or is it based on a 1- or 2-year fad?
    e. Do you stick with your philosophy and insert your players into it, or do you adapt to the players who are available?
    f. Is there a better way of doing what you are doing?
    g. Can you explain why you use or do something?
    h. Is what you do in practice sessions and games safe?
    i. Is your coaching philosophy compatible with your personality?
    j. Is there anything unsportsmanlike involved with your philosophy?
7. Eight coaching competencies (National Association for Sport and Physical Education, 2006):
    a. Philosophy and ethics
    b. Safety and injury prevention
    c. Physical conditioning
    d. Growth and development
    e. Teaching and communication
    f. Sport skills and tactics
    g. Organization and administration
    h. Evaluation

---

http://health.jbpub.com/book/prepare

Go to the web component of *Preparing the Successful Coach* at http://health.jbpub.com/book/prepare for web exercises and a suggested reading list.

Discussion Questions

1. How would you describe the characteristics of individuals you consider to be a good coach? A bad coach?

_____

_____

_____

2. What is the difference between how a good coach and a bad coach "carry themselves," both on and away from the playing arena?

_____

_____

_____

3. How would the following constituents describe a good coach?
    a. Current student-athletes?

_____

_____

_____

b. Former student-athletes?

_____

_____

c. Parents of student-athletes?

_____

_____

d. Coaches of the same sport within the conference?

_____

_____

e. Coaches of different sports at the same school?

_____

_____

f. Principals and other administrators?

_____

_____

g. Community members?

_____

_____

4. a. What are the components of a solid coaching philosophy?

_____

_____

b. How should such a philosophy balance winning and the development of quality young student-athletes? Provide examples of how these two ideas may be both congruent and antithetical.

_____

_____

c. How should such a philosophy include the mission or philosophy of the educational institution where the coach is employed?

_____

_____

_____

5. Hoch asks coaches to consider whether they adapt their philosophy for their players or insert their players into their philosophy. What are the advantages and disadvantages to both? When, or under what circumstances, might one answer truly be better?

_____

_____

_____

_____

6. Who wins games—coaches or players? Who loses games? How do coaches affect the outcomes of games? Do coaches affect the outcome of games more during practice or during the game?

_____

_____

_____

_____

7. Can a successful coach consistently have a losing record? Can an unsuccessful coach consistently win? Why or why not?

_____

_____

_____

_____

8. How much are perennial successful programs the result of a great coach as compared with the community's culture?

_____

_____

_____

_____

9. Do student-athletes play and work harder for good coaches? Do they consistently perform better for good coaches? Why or why not?

_____

_____

_____

_____

10. Does playing experience (minimum high school varsity) make one a better coach? Why or why not? How might playing experience at an advanced level (elite college and/or professional) help a coach? Hinder a coach? How might the recentness of the playing experience help or hinder a coach?

_____

_____

_____

11. a. When should a coach be dismissed? Can 1 year be enough to decide? Why or why not?

_____

_____

_____

_____

CHAPTER

3

Balancing Coaching with Other Professional Duties

Many school districts prefer to hire coaches who also teach in the district and give these individuals first preference in the hiring process. These individuals often are faced with a delicate balance between both their coaching and teaching duties and the general student population and student-athletes for which they are responsible.

Other coaches are not employed in the district and may have a full-time job outside of their coaching assignment. These individuals encounter a separate set of challenges while attempting to balance their passion for coaching with their job that "pays the bills." Challenges also exist for individuals who simultaneously may be a coach and a full-time college student.

This chapter investigates these balances. Suggestions are provided to perfect the balance between teaching and coaching. The discussion questions implicitly ask prospective coaches to consider what they owe the general student population in relation to their student-athletes. The questions also ask coaches to critique the communication during the interview process and to determine the balance in how teacher-coaches should be formally evaluated.

Five scenarios are presented. Two involve situations where your teaching duties conflict with your teaching responsibilities. Two are occurrences where a second job or college final exam interferes with your coaching assignment. The final scenario forces a coach to decide how he or she would vote, as a member of the teachers' union, on a strike that could impact the season.

Warm-Up

Here we introduce coaches to strategies to assist in perfecting the balance between coaching and teaching. Such strategies can potentially help the professional to avoid or to be prepared for potential situations that are either unpleasant or could result in disciplinary action.

1. Strategies to perfect the teacher-coach balance:
   a. Possess a complete understanding of your administration's expectations concerning this balance; do not leave any question unasked or unanswered.
   b. Communicate all potential conflicts to the administration as soon as possible.
   c. Communicate your decisions (if left up to you) in the event of a conflict in person and in a timely fashion to those who need to know.
   d. Realize you cannot make everyone happy; expect and understand one group of students to be upset.

e. Be leery of the precedent set and the message sent any time you place athletics over academics; always bear in mind you have a responsibility to the student-athletes and taxpayers to provide your classes with the best education possible.

http://health.jbpub.com/book/prepare

Go to the web component of *Preparing the Successful Coach* at http://health.jbpub.com/book/prepare for web exercises and a suggested reading list.

Discussion Questions

1. Are most teacher-coaches coaches who teach or teachers who coach? What is the difference? Can you identify some examples of when the dual roles may conflict?

_____

_____

_____

2. How does a teacher-coach implicitly and explicitly let his or her preference show?

_____

_____

_____

3. a. Can both jobs be done at an excellent level? Why or why not?

_____

_____

b. A stereotype may exist that coaches emphasize their game planning at the expense of preparing for classes. Is this fair?

_____

_____

c. Do teacher-coaches have a harder time proving themselves to their faculty colleagues? Why or why not?

_____

_____

4. Should coaching and teaching be separate positions under ideal circumstances? What are advantages and disadvantages with both situations? Why would administrators want their coaches to be teachers, preferably in their district?

_____

_____

_____

5. What should be the primary factors when deciding whether a teacher-coach should receive tenure? What percentage of the evaluation should come from teaching responsibilities? Coaching responsibilities?

_____

_____

_____

_____

6. a. Do principals have a responsibility during the interview to communicate the expectations both in the classroom and on the game field, and how the teacher-coach will subsequently be evaluated, during the interview process?

_____

_____

_____

b. Do prospective teacher-coaches have a responsibility to ensure the expectations are communicated?

_____

_____

_____

c. What questions should the prospective teacher-coach ask?

_____

_____

_____

7. What are the potential challenges for a coach having his or her student-athletes in class? Are teacher-coaches generalized to be tougher or more lenient with student-athletes enrolled in their classes?

_____

_____

_____

8. What are the potential challenges with teaching in one school district but coaching in a second district?

_____

_____

_____

_____

9. What should be communicated between a principal and coach who has a job outside the district before mutually agreeing on accepting or offering a coaching assignment?

_____

_____

_____

10. What should the off-season duties be for a coach who has a full-time job outside the district or who is a college student? Should he or she be given more leeway than coaches who are teachers in the district? Is that fair to the student-athletes? Why or why not?

_____

_____

_____

_____

Scenarios

1. Your history class is taking a unit exam. A student enters the class with a message for you that Coach Jones is on the phone in your office, returning your call concerning a scouting report on this evening's opponent. What do you do?

_____

_____

_____

2. You are the leading science teacher at your school. You have worked hard with several students on their science projects and teachers at your school typically attend the district science fair with their student participants. You are also the wrestling coach and your athletic director has scheduled a match for the same night. Neither event can be rescheduled, and you have a strong obligation to both groups. What do you do?

_____

_____

_____

3. You are an assistant manager at a local retail store. You want to begin a career in coaching and have been recently hired as the local high school's sophomore baseball coach. You have arranged both schedules so that conflicts should not exist. However, both your retail manager and the school expect to be the priority if a conflict surfaces. The high school principal went as far as indicating your evaluation and the decision to rehire you next year will be impacted by your ability to have a clear schedule. You are preparing for a home baseball game when your retail manager calls. Three of your coworkers have been injured in a car accident en route to work and the store is going to be short-staffed. The manager is calling you from a conference in another state, meaning you are in charge and are expected to go to the store to help cover. You cannot be both in the store and at the ball game and you must make a decision. One supervisor is going to be extremely unhappy. What do you do?

_____

_____

_____

4. You teach and coach at your school and are a member of the teachers' union. Tense negotiations are ensuing between the union and the school district, and a strike vote is looming. You firmly believe the union's demands are fair and in the best interest of you and your professional colleagues. However, pre-season practice begins in 2 weeks and a strike would mean your team would lose valuable instructional time. Your faculty colleagues are conducting a straw poll of whether or not to issue a notice to strike and wish to know where you stand. What are all the considerations of your decision? Where do you believe you would stand? Would you ever consider crossing a picket line to conduct practice? What would all the considerations be of such a decision?

_____

_____

_____

_____

5. You are a senior in college and also the local high school's softball coach. You were able to take all morning classes during your last semester so there have been no conflicts between your classes and your job. The final exam schedule has just been released, however, and you have a 3:15 exam at the same time you have a home softball game. Your instructor is not going to accommodate you, and taking a zero on the exam could result in you failing the course and not graduating. You do not have an adult assistant coach on whom you can rely. How do you handle this situation? What are all your options?

_____

_____

_____

_____

Practice Exercise

1. Identify your professional goals for each position you hold. Create separate lists, in rank order, for your coaching position and your other professional duties. Then combine the lists into one rank order. Where would your top coaching goal rank on your combined list? Your top goal unrelated to your coaching position? How would this new rank order translate into decisions you would make should a conflict arise between your coaching and other professional responsibilities? Share your thoughts with a colleague and critique each other's efforts.

_____

_____

_____

_____

_____

_____

CHAPTER

4

Balancing Coaching with Family and Personal Time

Coaches differ in their marital status, whether they have children, and their closeness to their parents, siblings, and extended family. Coaches also differ in their hobbies and their need for personal time. Coaches may experience difficulties effectively balancing coaching and family and coaching and other aspects of their personal lives.

This chapter looks at the time constraints and demands coaching places on family and personal time. Also provided are suggestions concerning this balance and a representation of the actual time demands coaches encounter. The discussion questions ask prospective coaches to ponder how supportive a role they want their family to play. The discussion questions also ask about the challenges of coaching family members and identify what family and other personal issues are acceptable to miss a practice or a game. The scenarios offer specific situations where a coach has to decide between his or her job and family demands. The practice exercises offer prospective coaches an opportunity to reflect on their own balance between coaching, family, and personal time.

Warm-Up

This section introduces coaches to strategies to assist in perfecting the balance between coaching and family life. A common theme identified is to avoid miscommunications. This section also identifies research on the time demands of coaches, affording readers a better concept of a snapshot in the day or week of the life of an in-season coach.

1. Ideas to help balance work and family (Graham, 2006):
   a. Planning
   b. Communication
   c. Hold family meetings
   d. Keep schedules that establish time for both professional and relationship goals
   e. Be willing to revise plans when necessary
   f. Understand what can be controlled and what cannot
   g. Keep a sense of humor
2. Time demands of North Carolina high school coaches (Gould, Chung, Smith, & White, 2006):
   a. Coaches work an average of 24.3 hours per week while in-season.
   b. Coaches are in-season an average of 17.6 weeks.
   c. Coaches work an average of 169.5 total hours in the off-season.

http://health.jbpub.com/book/prepare

Go to the web component of *Preparing the Successful Coach* at http://health.jbpub.com/book/prepare for web exercises and a suggested reading list.

Discussion Questions

1. How difficult is it to be both a great coach and a great family person?

_____

_____

_____

_____

2. a. What is the time commitment involved with being an in-season coach?

_____

_____

b. What are the commitments involved with being a member of a family? A parent? A spouse? A son or daughter? A sibling? A member of an extended family?

_____

_____

_____

c. How may conflict occur? Provide specific examples.

_____

_____

_____

3. a. How can the pressures of coaching affect a spouse/significant other? Children?

_____

_____

b. It has been stated that a coach's spouse or significant other knows what they are "getting into" regarding the time demands coaches face. Is this a fair statement?

_____

_____

_____

4. Is there pressure for a coach's family to behave a certain way, especially within the community?

_____

_____

_____

_____

5. What are advantages and disadvantages to coaches having their family at games? Does the community expect it?

_____

_____

_____

_____

6. How should a coach balance staying after practice and helping players improve with getting home to spend time with the family?

_____

_____

_____

_____

7. How easy or difficult is it to leave a tough loss at the office?

_____

_____

_____

_____

8. What are the advantages and disadvantages to coaches working effectively at home?

_____

_____

_____

_____

9. What challenges come with coaching your children, nieces, or nephews?

_____

_____

_____

_____

10. What family demands are acceptable reasons to miss practice? A game? Who should be involved in the decision whether or not to miss work for a family obligation?

_____

_____

_____

_____

11. Do female coaches have a responsibility to reasonably attempt to give birth to their children out of season? What other considerations exist for women regarding pregnancy and coaching?

_____

_____

_____

12. How many days are reasonable for a male coach to take off in-season when his wife or partner has a baby?

_____

_____

_____

13. What other aspects of personal life may impact or be hindered by coaching responsibilities? Would the following examples of non–family-related personal issues be acceptable for a coach to miss a practice? A game?

a. A dental emergency?

_____

_____

b. Elective surgery?

_____

_____

c. An appointment with a realtor concerning buying or selling a house?

_____

_____

d. An appointment with a loan officer concerning a loan?

_____

_____

e. To vote?

_____

_____

f. Can you identify other examples?

_____

_____

_____

Scenarios

1. Your spouse is being recognized as the "Employee of the Year" and a large banquet is being prepared in his or her honor. The banquet falls on the evening of a game. Your spouse attends several games a year and is supportive of your work; however, he or she expects you to miss a game to be at the banquet. What do you do?

_____

_____

_____

_____

2. Your daughter is the lead in the high school play. The play runs two consecutive weekends, but your team is scheduled to play during each performance. What do you do?

_____

_____

_____

_____

3. Your son is graduating from college. His graduation occurs simultaneously with a conference softball game. What do you do?

_____

_____

_____

_____

4. Your mother has been diagnosed with cancer and has been struggling for some time. She has suddenly taken a turn for the worst, and your brother calls to inform you the doctors believe her death is imminent and to implore you to get to the hospital. Your assistant coach and principal were apprised of this possibility at the beginning of the season, but your players were not. The next flight to your mother's hometown leaves at 4:15 p.m. Your team has practice today and to-morrow and a game the following day. How should you proceed?

_____

_____

_____

_____

5. You sustain serious internal injuries in an automobile accident and miss 1 week of practices and games. Your doctor prefers you wait 1 more week before returning to action, and your principal prefers you listen to the doctor. You are itching to return to the team and are willing to "tough it out." How should this situation be handled?

_____

_____

_____

_____

Practice Exercises

1. Create three separate lists. One list should include all the responsibilities you have as an adult in society. The second list should include all the things unrelated to coaching that are important to you. The third list should delineate your coaching responsibilities and the reasons you are passionate about your profession. Combine all three lists and arrange the items hierarchically by order of importance. Share your lists and thoughts with a colleague and have him or her ask questions on your priorities.

_____

_____

_____

_____

_____

_____

2. It has been said, "There will be crucial times in a person's life when he or she has to make a decision between work and family and the subsequent choice both defines who they are and cannot be taken back." Write a paragraph on how this statement may apply to your life. Include specific past or future examples of such decisions. Finally, articulate whether or not you agree with the statement. Share your thoughts with a colleague and mutually discuss your paragraphs.

_____

_____

_____

_____

_____

_____

References

Gould, D., Chung, Y., Smith, P., & White, J. (2006 September). Future directions in coaching life skills: Understanding high school coaches' views and needs. *Athletic Insight: The Online Journal of Sport Psychology, 8*(3). Retrieved November 9, 2006 from http://www.athleticinsight.com/Vol8Iss3/CoachingLifeSkills.htm.

Graham, J. (2006). Balancing work and family. Retrieved November 9, 2006 from University of Maine Cooperative Extension website at http://www.umext.maine.edu/onlinepubs/htmpubs/4186.htm.

EXERCISES 4.0

CHAPTER

5

Professional Advancement

It is rare for a coach to remain at the same institution throughout his or her career. Whether or not to change jobs can be a tough decision and can be stressful for all involved—the coach, the student-athletes, and the administration. Disconcerting situations can arise, even when communication is open and honest.

This chapter investigates the reasons coaches may desire to take another job and discusses the coaches' duty to their former student-athletes when they take another job. The discussion questions ask coaches to identify who they should and should not keep informed about their job search and how they should handle a situation when the fact they interviewed for a high-profile job becomes public. The discussion questions also investigate how close to the beginning of the season does it become unprofessional to accept another position.

The scenarios involve situations where a coach is playing his or her former team and where a head coach may lose one of his or her assistants to another job opportunity. A practice exercise provides an opportunity for a coach to contemplate his or her personal considerations when deciding to take a new job.

Warm-Up

This chapter introduces coaches to the reasons they may begin to explore different job opportunities. Most coaches will change jobs, either on their own accord or not, at some time during their coaching career. Also identified is a coach's obligation to his or her former administration and student-athletes when changing jobs on his or her own accord.

1. Reasons a coach may explore other job opportunities:
    a. Opportunity to work at a larger or more prestigious or financially sound school
    b. Higher salary and/or better benefits
    c. Opportunity to have a more favorable teaching assignment
    d. Opportunity to coach, or not coach, a second sport
    e. Opportunity to be closer to family
    f. Opportunity to be closer to hometown
    g. Spouse or significant other received an exciting job opportunity in a different community
    h. A sour relationship with the school's administration or the community
    i. The junior varsity, and/or junior high squad, does not appear to have much talent
    j. Opportunity to tackle a new challenge

2. A coach's obligations when he or she leaves, on his or her accord, to take another job:
   a. Contact the school administration in person.
   b. Contact your assistant coaches in person.
   c. Call a team meeting to announce your intentions to the players; contact as many student-athletes in person if such a meeting is not feasible.
   d. Expect people to be upset and do not overreact to negative responses.
   e. Do not criticize your players, program, or school once you leave.

> **http://health.jbpub.com/book/prepare**
>
> Go to the web component of *Preparing the Successful Coach* at http://health.jbpub.com/book/prepare for web exercises and a suggested reading list.

Discussion Questions

1. Critique the reasons a coach may explore other job opportunities provided above. Are there other reasons why a coach might explore other job opportunities?

_____

_____

_____

2. How should a coach balance loyalty to his or her personal goals, family and loved ones, and current student-athletes and administration?

_____

_____

_____

3. a. How close to the beginning of the season should a coach not accept another job? Does it matter if the coach perceives he or she will be fired at season's end?

_____

_____

   b. Is there ever a situation where a coach is justified leaving his or her job during the season? If so, provide an example. How about an assistant coach?

_____

_____

_____

4. Who should and should not a coach tell when he or she is actively looking for other employment? When should he or she inform those necessary?

_____

_____

_____

5. Interviewing for a high-profile job may become public. How should a coach handle such a situation with his or her current team? What challenges might a coach face if the school where he or she interviewed does subsequently not hire him or her?

_____

_____

_____

_____

6. Critique the background information concerning a coach's obligation when he or she leaves to take another job. How should a coach inform current players he or she has taken a new job? His or her employers? The media and the community at large?

_____

_____

_____

_____

7. How may the answers to the preceding question change if the coach is hired during the summer? How may the answer change if the coach does not leave on his or her own accord?

_____

_____

_____

_____

8. Do high school student-athletes truly understand how another job may be better than coaching them?

_____

_____

_____

_____

9. a. Are there a number of times a coach can inform the administration of his or her intent to seek different employment before it is time to move on? Why or why not?

_____

_____

b. Is an administration justified for not renewing someone's contract for the primary reason they believe the person is constantly looking to leave? Why or why not?

_____

_____

10. How should a coach answer the following direct questions from his or her supervisors, assuming the coach is in fact "keeping his or her eyes open"?
a. "Are you looking for another job?"

_____

_____

_____

b. "Are you committed to the program for the long term?"

_____

_____

_____

11. What does a head coach owe his or her assistants in helping them explore other job opportunities?

_____

_____

_____

_____

12. How, if at all, do any of the preceding answers change if the situation is at the college and not high school level?

_____

_____

_____

_____

13. Who should retain possession of scouting reports when a coach leaves one school and accepts a new job at another school—the coach or the school? How about game films?

_____

_____

_____

_____

Scenarios

1. You are the softball coach at your high school. You left a neighboring community after seven seasons. Your current team is now playing your previous employer in the regional championship. You left with a positive relationship with players, parents, and the administration. How should a coach handle the following incidents with people associated with his or her former job?
a. A parent comes up to you before the game wanting to chat.
b. A parent comes up to you before the game to criticize your replacement.
c. A group of former players walk past you but appear to be shy in not knowing what to say.

_____

_____

_____

2. You are the volleyball coach at your high school. Rosie is your assistant varsity and head junior varsity coach. A head-coaching job has recently opened at another school and Rosie is one of the finalists. Pre-season practice begins in 1 week and Rosie is sensitive to possibly leaving the program this late in the summer. She asks for your advice. How would you counsel her, balancing the needs of your program with this exciting opportunity for a friend?

_____

_____

_____

_____

3. You are the boy's basketball coach and history teacher at a high school located in a small community. You have worked hard to build the program during your four seasons and have earned the respect of the players and the community. It is summer and your team is entered in several team camps; this next year will bring some excitement and realistically the team should contend for its first conference championship in 44 years. You had not been looking for another job, but you receive a call on June 24 from the athletic director of a larger high school. They have an immediate need for a boy's high school basketball coach and history teacher and you are on their short list of candidates. The position would be at a larger program that has strong basketball tradition, has outstanding facilities, and has more assistant coaches to distribute the duties. The job would pay $15,000 more annually and the school is located just 30 minutes from your spouse's family and thus your children's grandparents. The larger community also offers more opportunities for employment for your spouse, an aspiring art teacher. How do you proceed?

_____

_____

_____

_____

Practice Exercise

1. Identify everything you would consider if offered a new job you found attractive. Which of these would be the predominant factors? With whom would you have to consult? Outline these answers and share them with a colleague.

_____

_____

_____

_____

_____

_____

_____

_____

_____

A Coach's Constituents

6

The Relationship with the Athletic Director and Other Head Coaches

Coaches can be described as autonomous. They make decisions concerning their teams and expect players to follow orders without questions. Head coaches can forget they are part of a chain of command, not at the top of it. They can also fail to appreciate their obligations to colleagues as a member of an entire athletic department.

This chapter looks at the relationships a head coach has with both the athletic director and fellow coaches. Tips for communication with athletic directors and orientation topics to discuss with them are also discussed.

The discussion questions critique the relationship with the athletic director. Readers are asked when it is necessary for a coach to go over the head of the athletic director. Coaches are also asked to articulate when and how their athletic director should stick up for them. The discussion questions ask coaches to consider their responsibilities toward their coaching colleagues and to determine how conflicts between head coaches are best settled.

The scenarios offer four situations depicting conflict between a head coach and the athletic director or fellow coaches. These conflicts involve student-athletes, scheduling, and summer camps. Prospective and current coaches are asked to decide the best solution.

Warm-Up

In this section we introduce coaches to the best practices concerning orientation to their new position, school, and coworkers. This section includes information more directly linked to the relationship between the coach and the athletic director. It also includes tips for how a coach should communicate concerns and expectations to the athletic director and situations when an athletic director needs to intervene with a coach.

1. Components of an orientation program for coaches (National Association for Sport and Physical Education, 2005):
   a. Provide an introduction to fellow coaches, athletic department personnel, and school administrators.
   b. Provide and discuss the policies and philosophies of the school.
   c. Provide and discuss the school's and program's coaches' code of conduct.
   d. Provide and discuss athlete eligibility guidelines and enforcement.
   e. Discuss the reasons for removal or suspension of a student-athlete.

© 2008 Jones and Bartlett Publishers, Inc.   www.jbpub.com

f. Provide and discuss the role of the coach in the college recruitment process.

g. Discuss the components of privacy issues related to personal health information.

h. Discuss the school's safety and emergency policies and procedures.

i. Discuss the school's requirements for athlete's pre-participation physicals and insurance coverage.

j. Discuss the coaches' responsibility concerning the purchase, storage and inventory of equipment.

2. Ideal orientation topics between an athletic director and a new coach:

   a. Current status of the team

   b. Current staff/assistant coaches

   c. Athletic director's subjective initial opinions on the new coach's strengths and weaknesses

   d. Where the responsibility of the coach ends and the athletic director begins

   e. The athletic department's philosophy

   f. Tryout policy

   g. Equipment storage

3. When an athletic director needs to intervene or offer assistance (Cardone, 2005):

   a. A coach demonstrates poor organizational skills

   b. A coach demonstrates poor communication skills

   c. A coach demonstrates behavior detrimental to the program

   d. A coach fails to notice important items

4. Tips for communicating with the athletic director:

   a. Respect your institution's chain of command.

   b. Realize the athletic director must balance the needs and interests of several sports.

   c. Realize the athletic director must balance the needs and interests of the coaching staff and the student-athletes.

   d. Trust your athletic director is "going to bat for you individually or for coaches collectively" until proven otherwise, realizing the athletic director has to answer to the principal or other top-level administrator.

   e. Treat the athletic director with the same respect you expect to receive from your assistant coaches.

   f. Learn what administrative duties are your responsibility and which are the athletic director's.

   g. Do not criticize an athletic director's decision you disagree with to student-athletes and/or their parents.

   h. Admit when you make a mistake or did not follow the correct procedure.

   i. Ask for clarification toward any policies or regulations for which you are unclear.

---

http://health.jbpub.com/book/prepare

Go to the web component of *Preparing the Successful Coach* at http://health.jbpub.com/book/prepare for web exercises and a suggested reading list.

Discussion Questions

1. Describe the ideal working relationship between the coach and the athletic director.

_____

_____

_____

_____

© 2008 Jones and Bartlett Publishers, Inc.   www.jbpub.com

2. How should a coach expect the athletic director to stick up for him or her if the need arises?

_____

_____

_____

3. How should a coach expect the athletic director to mediate a dispute between a coach and a player, two constituents for whom athletic directors are responsible?

_____

_____

_____

4. How should a head coach expect the athletic director to mediate a dispute between him or her and an assistant coach? Does it matter if the assistant coach has superseded the head coach in the chain of command?

_____

_____

_____

5. How should a head coach expect an athletic director to mediate disputes between head coaches?

_____

_____

_____

6. When might it be necessary to go over the athletic director's head?

_____

_____

_____

7. What are the advantages and disadvantages of simultaneously being a coach and an athletic director?

_____

_____

_____

8. How should the following duties be balanced between the head coach and the athletic director?
   a. Scheduling of non-conference games

_____

_____

_____

b. Scheduling of practice times

_____

_____

_____

c. The hiring, promotion, and firing of assistant coaches

_____

_____

_____

d. The budget

_____

_____

_____

e. Travel arrangements

_____

_____

_____

f. Ordering of uniforms and equipment

_____

_____

_____

9. a. What is a head coach's responsibility toward his or her fellow head coaches within the athletic department?

_____

_____

_____

b. Should a head coach make an honest attempt to attend a home contest for every sport in the school to show support?

_____

_____

_____

c. How else can a coach demonstrate support of fellow coaches and their programs?

_____

_____

_____

d. When should a coach go to the athletic director with a complaint about a colleague, when should they attempt to solve the problem themselves, and when should he or she drop it? Provide specific examples.

_____

_____

_____

e. What should a coach do when one colleague approaches him or her with critical remarks about another colleague?

_____

_____

_____

10. What should a coach do upon discovering a fellow coach is making critical remarks about his or her program?

_____

_____

_____

Scenarios

1. You are the head football coach at your school. The athletic director is the boy's soccer coach. You know definitively he is attempting to persuade some of your best student-athletes to play soccer instead of football. What should you do?

_____

_____

_____

2. A player's parent has requested a meeting with you and the athletic director. At this meeting the parent accuses you of swearing at her daughter. You tell the athletic director the truth: You did not do this. Both you and the parent are adamant in the versions surrounding the allegation. How would you expect the athletic director to address this scenario?

_____

_____

_____

3. You are the head wrestling coach at your school. Last night's boy's basketball home game was canceled due to inclement weather. The athletic director rescheduled the game for tonight. The wrestling meet originally scheduled for tonight has been moved to the practice gym. You are livid both for having to host your meet in the practice gym and that you were not allowed to provide input before a decision was made. What should you do?

_____

_____

_____

4. You are the girls' tennis coach at your school. You contact the athletic director in February to schedule the courts for your annual summer camp, held the third week in June every year for the past 6 years. The new boy's tennis coach was unaware of the procedures to reserve the courts for summer camps and inadvertently scheduled the camp the same week as yours. The publicity for both camps has already been released. You expect the athletic director to take your side because you are the one who correctly followed procedure. Instead, the athletic director implores both tennis coaches to "work something out." How do you approach both the boy's tennis coach and the athletic director to resolve this situation?

_____

_____

_____

Practice Exercise

1. Create questions you would ask both the athletic director and fellow head coaches during a job interview. What types of responses do you hope to receive and why would the answers to these questions be important to you? How might the answers impact your decision to accept a position? Share your thoughts with a colleague and critique each other's efforts.

_____

_____

_____

_____

_____

_____

_____

_____

References

Cardone, D. (2005). Rookie at bat. *Athletic Management, 17*(4), 41–48.

National Association for Sport and Physical Education. (2005). Program orientation for high school sport coaches. *Strategies, 18*(6), 20.

CHAPTER

7

The Assistant Coach

An assistant coach can be both a big asset and a liability for a program. Assistant coaches vary in their experience, knowledge, motives, and aspirations. Head coaches must balance each of these components and the assistant coach's overall working conditions with the overall good of the program. A good head coach hires and trains quality assistants and then delegates the proper authority to them. A head coach must decide what duties he or she is comfortable delegating to assistants. Head coaches must then properly communicate these responsibilities and be willing to let their assistants learn through experience.

This chapter describes the ideal characteristics of an assistant coach, components of an assistant coach's evaluation, and considerations when hiring volunteer coaches. The discussion questions investigate the assistant coach's multiple roles and the several different potential interactions he or she has with head coaches and the team. The discussion questions also provide insight into how destructive a poor assistant coach can be.

Six scenarios are presented. They cover situations where your assistant coaches have demonstrated disrespect toward you or a student-athlete and where an assistant coach encounters a student-athlete violating team rules.

The chapter concludes with two practice exercises. The first allows coaches to decide what tasks they are comfortable delegating to an assistant coach. The second practice exercise forces coaches to self-reflect on their ability to delegate authority.

Warm-Up

This chapter offers coaches authors' opinions on the characteristics of a good assistant coach. Good assistant coaches can become a huge advantage to a program and to a head coach. We also offer suggestions to coaches for hiring volunteers as assistant coaches.

1. Characteristics of a good assistant coach (Sabock & Sabock, 2005):
   a. Loyalty
   b. Teacher and technician
   c. Knowledge of the sport
   d. Enthusiasm
   e. Initiative
   f. Dependability
   g. Sound philosophy
   h. Desire to be a head coach
   i. Playing experience
   j. Willingness to attend clinics
   k. Rapport with athletes

© 2008 Jones and Bartlett Publishers, Inc.   www.jbpub.com

    l. Ability to serve as liaison between the players and head coach

    m. Willingness to work

    n. Willingness to contribute ideas

    o. Motivation

    p. Flexibility

2. Additional characteristics of a good assistant coach:

    a. A complement to the head coach's style and personality

    b. Ability to specialize on a facet of the game (e.g., pitching, goal keeping)

    c. Capable of doing anything in the head coach's absence

    d. A "yes" person in front of the team but willing to appropriately challenge the head coach in private

    e. Ability to have their suggestions rejected without inhibiting their ability to continue making them

    f. A comprehension of the program's direction

3. Considerations for hiring volunteer coaches (Cardone, 2000):

    a. Conduct the same background checks as you would a paid assistant.

    b. Have the aspiring volunteer interview with the athletic director.

    c. Thoroughly discuss their role on the coaching staff.

    d. Have the aspiring volunteer attend the pre-season coaches meeting.

    e. Examine their motives for wishing to be on the staff. Be leery of parents, hometown heroes, or individuals who may truly want to be the head coach.

4. Components of an assistant coach's evaluation (Cardone, 2006):

    a. Relationship with coaching staff

    b. Relationship with players

    c. Loyalty to the program

    d. Professional growth

http://health.jbpub.com/book/prepare

Go to the web component of *Preparing the Successful Coach* at http://health.jbpub.com/book/prepare for web exercises and a suggested reading list.

Discussion Questions

1. What are the responsibilities of an assistant coach? Which of these are the primary responsibilities?

_____

_____

_____

2. What are the head coach's responsibilities in training and evaluating an assistant coach?

_____

_____

_____

3. What are the advantages and disadvantages of having a formal job description for assistant coaches?

_____

_____

_____

4. What are the advantages and disadvantages of having an assistant coach have complete control of a group of players who play one position? Complete control over the offense or defense?

_____

_____

_____

_____

5. Is having a weak assistant coach better or worse than having no assistant coach?

_____

_____

_____

6. a. Describe the fine line an assistant has to walk between being an advocate for the players and an employee of the head coach.

_____

_____

_____

b. How can this line get crossed?

_____

c. What is a head coach's responsibility when it does?

_____

_____

_____

7. a. Sabock and Sabock describe loyalty as a good characteristic of an assistant coach. What are the components of loyalty?

_____

_____

b. How should a head coach expect his or her assistant coach to balance loyalty to the program and the assistant's own professional aspirations?

_____

_____

8. a. How should an assistant coach handle a situation where a student-athlete comes to him or her complaining about playing time?

_____

_____

b. What if the assistant believes the student-athlete should be playing more?

_____

_____

_____

c. What if the assistant knows the head coach has little confidence in this student-athlete?

_____

_____

_____

9. a. Are there situations an assistant coach should be empowered to discipline?

_____

_____

_____

b. Should a head coach expect to be informed of every discipline scenario his or her assistants encounter, or can assistants handle some things without the head coach's knowledge? What may be some examples of such things an assistant coach can handle by him- or herself?

_____

_____

_____

10. a. Should a hierarchy exist when a team has more than one assistant coach? Why or why not?

_____

_____

_____

b. What components should be included when determining a hierarchy? Should the assistant coach with the longest tenure automatically be the top assistant? Why or why not?

_____

_____

_____

11. What is better to have—an assistant with desire or no desire to be a head coach? Does this impact how he or she is utilized?

_____

_____

_____

_____

12. a. How much freedom should a coach give the junior varsity coach to incorporate his or her own offensive and defensive strategies?

_____

_____

_____

b. What is the balance between running a program and allowing for the professional development of assistant coaches?

_____

_____

_____

13. a. When should a head coach allow an assistant coach to make a mistake and learn from it, and when should he or she intervene to prevent the mistake?

_____

_____

b. What is the appropriate way for the head coach to handle a situation when an assistant coach has made a mistake?

_____

_____

14. What expectations should a coach have of assistant coaches in the summer? How might the conditions of their contract matter?

_____

_____

_____

15. a. Should a coach give the assistant coach who stabbed him or her in the back a second chance?

_____

_____

b. Can an assistant coach be a bigger cancer to a team than a disgruntled player? Why or why not?

_____

_____

16. How should a coach handle the situation where an assistant coach becomes disgruntled with his or her role?

_____

_____

17. How should a coach handle a situation where an assistant coach disrespects him or her in front of the team?

_____

_____

18. a. What say should each of the following constituents have on the hiring of an assistant coach/faculty member: the head coach, the athletic director, or the principal?

_____

_____

_____

b. How about the hiring of an assistant coach who will not be on the faculty?

_____

_____

19. What say should each of the following constituents have on the disciplining or termination of an assistant coach: the head coach, the athletic director, or the principal?

_____

_____

_____

20. What are the potential opportunities and threats for a young and relatively inexperienced head coach to have a more experienced and older assistant or someone similar in age and experience?

_____

_____

_____

21. What special considerations exist for a volunteer coach? A coach who is a student-teacher? A coach who is a student in the school?

_____

_____

_____

_____

Scenarios

1. An assistant coach witnesses a student-athlete out after team curfew. Alcohol, obnoxious behavior, or vandalism is not involved. How should the assistant handle this violation?

_____

_____

_____

2. Three student-athletes, all starters, approach the assistant coach with a complaint. They disagree with the significant amount of playing time the head coach is giving a teammate and believe other teammates should have increased roles. The assistant agrees with the players' assessment but knows the head coach strongly disagrees. How should the assistant handle this situation?

_____

_____

_____

3. You are a head football coach and are primarily involved with the offense. Last season you promoted one of your assistants to the title of defensive coordinator; this individual already had primary duties with the defense and you wished to reward his effort. Unfortunately, you did not effectively communicate your expectations and guidelines for a defensive coordinator and conflicts, sometimes visible to players, ensued concerning alignments and personnel. You also believe this coach made the defense "his team" and overall team chemistry suffered as a result. How do you approach this next season with this individual?

_____

_____

_____

4. You are a head softball coach and also serve as the third base coach. You wave in the tying home run and the player is thrown out at the plate to end the inning, leaving your best hitter on deck. Your assistant coach, who also serves as the first base coach, is staring at you in disbelief. She continues to shake her head and mutter under her breath while returning to the dugout. She is clearly demonstrating disrespect. How, and when, do you approach this situation?

_____

_____

_____

5. A long-time friend and coaching colleague contacts you. She informs you that she attended a coaching clinic last weekend where your assistant coach was being overly critical of your ability as a head coach. You have no reason to distrust your friend. How do you handle this situation?

_____

_____

_____

6. Your team is practicing drills. You have a group of players on one side of the playing area and your assistant coach has another group of student-athletes. Suddenly your assistant coach is yelling and screaming at one of your players. He is not swearing or physically accosting the student-athlete, but the situation is getting out of control and has become a distraction. You do not want to undermine your assistant coach in front of the players, but you also believe he needs to get control of himself. You do not yet know what caused the outburst. How do you handle this situation—both now and later?

_____

_____

_____

Practice Exercises

1. Identify all the tasks you would like your top assistant coach to complete for you throughout a season. Include practice, game, and administrative duties and be specific. Share these with a colleague and ask each other questions, including whether you would want to work as an assistant coach in this role.

_____

_____

_____

_____

_____

_____

_____

2. Review the roles you have assumed in the various group efforts you have encountered. This could include class projects, work duties, athletic responsibilities, and so on. Assess your personality in relation to your recollections. Are you someone who has problems delegating responsibility? Trusting colleagues or teammates to do their share? Confronting individuals who have not done their fair share? Based on your answers, are you someone you would want to work for as an assistant coach? Share your thoughts with a colleague and have a conversation surrounding your analysis.

_____

_____

_____

_____

_____

_____

_____

_____

References

Cardone, D. (2000). For the love of it. _Athletic Management, 12_(6), 41–44.

Cardone, D. (2006). Exceeds expectations. _Athletic Management, 18_(5), 51–57.

Sabock, R.J., & Sabock, M.D. (2005). _Coaching: A realistic perspective_ (8th ed.). Lanham, MD: Rowman & Littlefield Publishers, Inc.

EXERCISE 7.0

8

Parent–Coach Relationships

The coach–parent relationship and parental involvement in their children's sporting lives are often stereotyped as negative. These stereotypes are often generated by increased news accounts of poor parental behavior and attacks against coaches by parents.

Overlooked are the positive interactions a coach has with parents. Barton and Stewart (2006) describe the parent–coach relationship either as helpful and supportive or stressful and frustrating. Effective communication and established guidelines can help coaches minimize the negative experiences and establish positive ones.

This chapter reviews different classifications of parents, characteristics parents want in their children's coaches, and rules for effective parent–coach communication. The discussion questions ask what characterizes an appropriate relationship with a parent and how a coach's age may impact it. The questions also ask coaches to consider how much access parents should have to their sons and daughters during practice and games. Five scenarios depict potential conflicts with parents and ask prospective coaches to ponder the ramifications of different decisions.

Warm-Up

Here coaches are introduced to suggestions for creating positive relationships with the often-maligned group of parents. Two sets of expectations are provided: what parents expect from coaches in the form of communication and what coaches expect from parents. Also included are what is and is not appropriate for parents to discuss with coaches as well as overall rules for coach–parent interaction.

1. Communication parents should expect from a coach:
   a. Philosophy of the coach
   b. Locations and times of all practices and contests
   c. Procedures should their child be injured during participation
   d. Discipline that results in the denial of their child's participation
   e. Expectations the coach has for your son or daughter, as well as other players on the team
   f. Team requirements, including fees, special equipment needed, school and team rules, and off-season expectations

2. Communication coaches should expect from parents:
   a. Notification of any schedule conflicts well in advance
   b. Specific concern in regard to a coach's philosophy or expectations
   c. Concerns regarding their son or daughter expressed directly to the coach at the appropriate time and place

3. Appropriate concerns to discuss with coaches:

  a. The treatment of your child, mentally and physically

  b. Ways to help your child improve

  c. Concerns about your child's behavior

4. Issues not appropriate to discuss with coaches (Iowa High School Athletic Association, n.d.; Workman, 2005):

  a. Playing time

  b. Team strategy

  c. Play calling

  d. Other student-athletes

5. Rules of parent–coach communication:

  a. Playing time, team strategy, and other players are not discussed.

  b. Procedures should be established for contacting a coach at home.

  c. Parents should respect the chain of command—matters should be brought to the coach's attention before the athletic director or other school officials.

  d. Potentially negative interaction should not occur after a contest.

  i. Coaches should be prepared to walk away, or in extreme cases call for security, after politely reiterating this policy.

  e. Official meetings with parents, and any unofficial meetings that warrant it, should be documented.

6. Parental preferences in coaching characteristics (Barton & Stewart, n.d.):

  a. Fairness and honesty in dealing with athletes

  b. Ability to teach well

  i. Know how to sequence learning

  ii. Give feedback

  iii. Create a positive environment

  c. Commitment to developing sportsmanship

---

http://health.jbpub.com/book/prepare

Go to the web component of *Preparing the Successful Coach* at http://health.jbpub.com/book/prepare for web exercises and a suggested reading list.

Discussion Questions

1. a. Should coaches have pre-season meetings with parents? Individually or as a group? Why or why not?

_____

_____

_____

b. Should such meetings be mandatory for parents to attend? Why or why not?

_____

_____

_____

c. Should the student-athletes be included at the initial coach–parent meeting? Why or why not?

_____

_____

_____

_____

2. Should practices be closed to parents? Why or why not?

_____

_____

_____

_____

3. How "parent-friendly" should a coach be? Should a coach accept an invitation to dinner or a drink from a parent? What are the considerations?

_____

_____

_____

_____

4. How may a coach's age affect his or her relationship with parents? Whether or not a coach has children the same age as his or her student-athletes?

_____

_____

_____

_____

5. What are some of the possible positives and challenges for a coach to have friends or colleagues whose children become student-athletes?

_____

_____

_____

_____

6. How can parents be an addition to the program?

_____

_____

_____

_____

7. How much of a coach's responsibility should it be to organize the parents who want to help in productive ways (car pools to practice, bringing snacks, etc.)?

_____

_____

_____

8. How should a coach handle a situation when a parent approaches him or her in a confrontational manner, both during and after the confrontation?

_____

_____

_____

9. Should a coach approach parents who place so much pressure on their children it affects performance?

_____

_____

_____

10. How much do bad parent–coach relationships spill into bad player–coach relationships?

_____

_____

_____

11. a. Should coaches allow parents to talk with their children during games?

_____

_____

b. How about between games of a double header or a tournament?

_____

_____

c. When should student-athletes be released to their parents after the game?

_____

_____

12. Should coaches be expected to take phone calls at home from parents?

_____

_____

_____

13. How should a coach handle receiving a phone call at home from a parent when it has been established parents should not call him or her there? Receiving a personal visit while at home?

_____

_____

_____

14. a. What are the considerations before a coach would ask a parent permission to record a meeting between them?

_____

_____

b. Why might a coach want a recording of the meeting?

_____

_____

c. Should a coach insist on recording meetings? Why or why not?

_____

_____

15. What should a head coach consider before accepting a parent as a volunteer assistant? Should a coach ask the input of the son or daughter?

_____

_____

_____

_____

Scenarios

1. John's parents are upset with his playing time and have scheduled a meeting with you. It is your opinion John has talent but continually gets out-hustled in practice and has a disruptive attitude. How do you convey this at the meeting?

_____

_____

_____

_____

2. Lisa, your softball catcher, comes to you between innings of your game. She believes the pitcher is constantly shaking her off because she is taking her signs from her father sitting in the bleachers behind home plate. What do you do?

_____

_____

_____

_____

3. Mark's parents arrive at today's practice. They bring their lawn chairs and sit and watch the entire practice without disruption. What do you do?

_____

_____

_____

_____

4. Monique approaches you during half-time of the team's basketball game. She complains that Amanda's parents are criticizing her (Monique) play during the game and it is upsetting her. You have not heard this because the stands are on the other side of the court; however, Monique's claim does not surprise you. Monique wants you to ask Amanda's parents to quit vocalizing their criticism, something you would prefer to do in a different setting than at half-time. What do you do?

_____

_____

_____

_____

5. Maria and Phil have been your neighbors for several years. Your relationship with them has always been cordial, and you often chatted with them. Their daughter, Pamela, now plays on your varsity volleyball team. These chats have now become a forum for Maria and Phil to subtly voice their opinions on the team, including gossip of off-the-court behaviors of Pamela's teammates. You cannot ascertain their intent in providing you this information. What do you do?

_____

_____

_____

_____

Practice Exercise

1. Prepare an outline of an agenda for a pre-season meeting you would have with parents. What would you include? What would you not include? What would you reserve for individual meetings with parents? Share your thoughts with a colleague and critique each other's efforts.

_____

_____

_____

_____

_____

_____

_____

References

Barton, C., & Stewart, C. (n.d.). Coaches' Info Service: Sport Science Information For Coaches. *Parental expectation of coaches: Closing the communication gap.* Retrieved November 9, 2006 from http://coachesinfo.com/category/becoming_a_better_coach/363.

Iowa High School Athletic Association. (n.d.). *Conduct counts: The parent and coach/advisor relationship.* Retrieved November 9, 2006 from http://www.iahsaa.org/ParCrel.doc.

Workman, J. (2005). *Tremont junior/senior high school Turks parent/coach communication* [Brochure]. Tremont, IL: Author.

CHAPTER

9

The Relationship with the Junior High, Middle School, and Other Amateur Sports Programs

High school student-athletes often play at the junior high or middle school level. These student-athletes enter their high school coach's program with skills and strategies previously taught. The specifics may not be similar to the high school coach's instruction and goals.

Some high schools have multiple feeder junior highs that may include different school districts. Other communities have one junior high feeding into one high school. This chapter asks how much input a high school coach should have on the junior high program and what, if any, specific responsibilities a high school coach has toward the junior high team.

High school student-athletes also often play on recreation league, club sport, or other amateur teams unaffiliated with a school program. Such programs may beget a different set of challenges for coaches. This chapter's discussion questions review some of these challenges.

The ideal communication between the high school and junior high programs is described. Three scenarios are presented. These include situations where high school coaches and either junior high or amateur coaches have philosophical differences. Two practice exercises ask coaches to prepare an agenda for initial meetings with the new junior high and club coach, respectively.

Warm-Up

In this section coaches are introduced to the desired communication between the high school coach and the junior high or middle school coach. The recommendations also include how a high school coach can have an effective relationship with local club teams. The successful coach is able to have productive relationships with both groups.

1. Effective communication between the junior high and high school programs and coaches:
   a. The high school coach should communicate the role he or she envisions for the junior high program, including specifics on strategies, skill development, and camps.
   b. The high school and junior high school coach should communicate on what, if any, role the high school coach should have in the junior high program, including guest visits to practices and games.

© 2008 Jones and Bartlett Publishers, Inc.   www.jbpub.com

c. The interview and hiring process should explicitly delineate if there is a formal official relationship between the two programs.

d. The junior high coach should be allowed some dissent, dependent on the official hierarchical structure.

---

http://health.jbpub.com/book/prepare

Go to the web component of *Preparing the Successful Coach* at http://health.jbpub.com/book/prepare for web exercises and a suggested reading list.

Discussion Questions

1. a. Describe the ideal relationship between the junior high or middle school program and the high school program.

_____

_____

_____

b. Is it different if more than one junior high feeds into the high school? Why or why not?

_____

_____

_____

2. Is the junior high program's primary purpose to serve as a feeder system for the high school program? How should this be balanced with the junior high program maintaining its own identity?

_____

_____

_____

_____

3. How much input should the high school varsity coach have in the following areas of the junior high program?

a. The hiring and firing of coaches

_____

_____

b. Selecting a team

_____

_____

c. Playing time

_____

_____

d. Scheduling

_____

_____

_____

e. Offensive and defensive strategies

_____

_____

_____

f. Teaching of fundamentals

_____

_____

_____

4. a. Should the junior high be expected to run the same offense and defense used at the high school?

_____

_____

_____

b. Should they execute the same fundamentals, such as the baseball swing or volleyball pass? Why or why not?

_____

_____

_____

5. Should the high school coach attend the junior high games? Vice versa?

_____

_____

_____

6. What are advantages and disadvantages of having the same person coaching both the junior high and high school teams?

_____

_____

_____

7. What should be done with the student-athlete who does not contribute much at the junior high level but has the potential to do so at the high school level (such as a tall but uncoordinated athlete)?

_____

_____

_____

8. Is a winning junior high program necessary to have a winning high school program? Why or why not?

_____

_____

_____

© 2008 Jones and Bartlett Publishers, Inc. www.jbpub.com

9. With whom should the junior high coach communicate if they have problems working alongside the high school coach? How may it matter if the schools are or are not in the same school district?

_____

_____

_____

_____

10. a. What is the ideal relationship between the high school coach and a recreation league, club sport, or other amateur sport coach?

_____

_____

_____

b. How does the fact the recreation league coach/club sport coach is not an employee of a school district make this relationship different?

_____

_____

_____

11. What are the opportunities and detriments club and other amateur sports afford coaches? Student-athletes?

_____

_____

_____

_____

12. What are the advantages and disadvantages to student-athletes who play one position or learn one style with a high school coach only to play a different position or learn different strategies with an amateur sport coach?

_____

_____

_____

13. What are the advantages and disadvantages of the high school coach serving as a recreation league coach for the same athletes (where allowed by high school state association guidelines)?

_____

_____

_____

Scenarios

1. You are a high school baseball coach. Several of your players play for the local American Legion team in the summer. Every year the Legion coach teaches your pitchers different mechanics than you did. You believe that receiving two separate forms of instruction limits their progress. You cannot realistically force your players to do things your way when pitching for a summer team not affiliated with the school's program. How should this situation be handled?

_____

_____

_____

_____

2. You are a high school coach who has worked well with the junior high coaches for your sport in the past. A new coach has been hired who politely informs you they do not believe in your offensive and defensive strategies and plan on teaching the skills and schemes they want. They add their vision for the junior high program is not one of a feeder program for the high school. How should this situation be handled?

_____

_____

_____

_____

3. You are a high school coach of a sport that has a local club team. You believe the club coach teaches strategies and skills that are unethical, against the rules, and potentially dangerous. How should this situation be handled?

_____

_____

_____

_____

Practice Exercises

1. You are a high school coach preparing for an initial meeting with the new junior high coach of the same sport. Prepare an agenda of items you wish to discuss. Share these with a colleague and critique each other's efforts.

_____

_____

_____

_____

_____

_____

_____

_____

2. You are a high school coach preparing for an initial meeting with your community's new club coach in the same sport. Prepare an agenda of items you wish to discuss. Share these with a colleague and critique each other's efforts.

_____

_____

_____

_____

_____

_____

_____

_____

CHAPTER

10

Other Constituents

Chapters 6 through 9 identified several of the constituents coaches are responsible to interact with on a regular basis. This includes the athletic director, other head coaches, assistant coaches, and parents. The junior high, middle school, and club program coaches are also other individuals head coaches may have to work and build relationships with during their careers.

There are other individuals as well coaches are responsible to interact with, depending on the particular community, sport, or school. These include booster clubs and local business persons as well as the community at large and the media.

Booster clubs often receive negative publicity, but they also offer many positives. The ideal situation is one where the booster club supports, not interferes with, the operation of the program (Appenzeller, 1993). High schools may have regulations as to who controls booster club business and raised monies. Coaches may or may not have an important role. This chapter's questions and scenarios discuss the coach's different roles and relationships with the booster club. The questions also spotlight the role of the coach in other fundraising pursuits. A practice exercise asks coaches to articulate their ideals concerning booster clubs and fundraising.

Coaches in smaller communities or in towns with one high school may face pressure from community members and local businesses. These pressures go beyond wins and losses and into attendance at community functions and where a coach purchases goods and services. This chapter's questions and scenarios pursue these issues.

An important responsibility of coaches, and one in which they are often not specifically trained, is working with the media. Coaches are responsible for reporting scores and working cooperatively with the media to enhance their student-athlete's exposure. Sometimes the relationship with the media is not always positive.

This chapter looks at the coach's responsibility with the media and whether the coach can and should use the media to their advantage. The discussion questions look at how student-athletes interact with the media and if coaches should curtail them. A scenario is presented where a coach has to perform "damage control" after a player makes inappropriate comments to the media, and a practice exercise prepares the coach for an interview setting.

Warm-Up

This section introduces coaches to information relevant to three separate issues. The first piece offers coaches advice on how to prepare for media interviews. The second categorizes the individuals who are involved with booster clubs and with whom coaches have the responsibility to interact. The third offers coaches fundraising tips.

1. Preparing the coach for an interview (Helitzer, 1999):
   a. Use mock interviews to become familiar with what to expect, including the reporter's tone.
   b. Rehearse questions and practice answering them positively.
   c. Inject points you want to inject—make the interview work for you.
   d. Do not offer off the record quotes or comments.
   e. Do not use lingo or acronyms.
   f. Be enthusiastic.
   g. Realize you do not control the final story/interview segment.
2. Categories of individuals involved with booster clubs (Sabock & Sabock, 2005):
   a. Those with a genuine interest in high school sports
   b. Parents of high school athletes
   c. Those who like to be associated with athletics and coaches
   d. Former coaches who want a forum to express their unhappiness
3. Tips for fundraising (Appenzeller, 1993):
   a. Be program specific.
   b. Establish a list of potential donors.
   c. Meet Internal Revenue Service standards.
   d. Use projects that have been successful previously.
   e. Acknowledge every donation.

http://health.jbpub.com/book/prepare

Go to the web component of *Preparing the Successful Coach* at http://health.jbpub.com/book/prepare for web exercises and a suggested reading list.

Discussion Questions

1. What are the positive and negative aspects of booster clubs?

_____

_____

_____

_____

2. Should booster clubs be for the entire athletic department or sport specific? What are the advantages and disadvantages of both situations?

_____

_____

_____

3. a. What role should the coach have with the booster club?

_____

_____

   b. How about a coach's significant other?

_____

_____

_____

4. a. Who should be responsible for deciding how raised monies will be spent—the coach, the athletic director and/or school administrators, or the booster club?

_____

_____

_____

b. What other fundraising opportunities exist outside of booster clubs? Who should be responsible for deciding how these raised monies should be spent?

_____

_____

_____

c. What is the coach's ideal role in fundraising?

_____

_____

_____

d. What are the characteristics of someone adept at this role?

_____

_____

_____

5. What should a coach convey to booster club leaders in an initial meeting?

_____

_____

_____

_____

6. a. Should coaches receive bonus payments from the booster club?

_____

_____

_____

b. How should a coach respond to such an offer?

_____

_____

_____

7. Is there an expectation a coach will live in the community in which he or she works? What are the advantages and disadvantages of doing so?

_____

_____

_____

8. Is there an expectation a coach will attend community functions, such as festivals and parades? How much should a coach alter his or her personal plans to accommodate such expectations?

_____

_____

_____

9. Is there an expectation a coach will purchase goods and services from local vendors? How much should a coach alter his or her personal plans and finances to accommodate such expectations?

_____

_____

_____

_____

10. a. What is the potential relationship between a coach purchasing goods and services from local vendors and local businesses financially supporting the team through advertisements and sponsorships?

_____

_____

_____

b. Should a coach pay special attention to purchasing locally from those businesses that financially support the program?

_____

_____

_____

11. Should coaches use the media to inflate or deflate player egos? Why or why not?

_____

_____

_____

_____

12. What is the coach's responsibility to interact and cooperate with the media?

_____

_____

_____

_____

13. Should a coach limit the media access to their student-athletes?

_____

_____

_____

_____

14. a. Should coaches attempt to curtail their student-athletes' comments to the media?

_____

_____

b. Should a coach allow a student-athlete capable of putting their foot in their mouth to do so and subsequently learn a lesson, or should a coach act preventively?

_____

_____

_____

c. How should a coach respond when a player has made an inappropriate remark to the media?

_____

_____

15. How much do student-athletes follow the media reports on them? Do they believe what they see, hear, or read? Do statements from opponents truly motivate them?

_____

_____

_____

16. How much should coaches promote a player through the media? Discourage the media to hype a player? What might be reasons a coach does both?

_____

_____

_____

_____

Scenarios

1. You are the head football coach at your school. The booster club supports all sports, but tradition dictates the football coach is the featured speaker at their annual pork chop dinner. Prominent booster club members unsuccessfully lobbied to have you fired after your team missed the playoffs last year. You have been invited to speak at this year's dinner. Should you accept the invitation? If so, should you address the matter during your speech? Why or why not? How do you handle the situation?

_____

_____

_____

2. You are a tennis coach at a school that does not have established fundraising guidelines. You approached some local businesses and asked them for donations to help offset the traveling costs your student-athletes incur to participate in summer camps. The booster club president is furious you are "hitting up" some of the same donors the booster club traditionally asks for money. They are asking you to either return the money to the businesses or submit the money to the booster club. The club officially represents the entire athletic department, but historically the funds are distributed to the football, boy's basketball, girl's basketball, and cheerleading squads. How do you handle this situation? How could you have handled it differently before soliciting donations?

_____

_____

_____

3. You would like to resurface your driveway. A well-respected company from a town 35 minutes away can do the job for $5,400. The most respected contractor in your community gave you a bid for $7,100. He and his wife purchase advertisements for local sports calendars and radio broadcast time. Which bid do you select and why?

_____

_____

_____

_____

4. You are in the process of accepting a coaching and teaching position in a school district 20 minutes from where you currently reside. Your spouse remains employed in this community and your children are well adjusted in the school district. You have no real intention of moving, and the situation was not discussed during your interview. However, on the day you are to sign your contract the principal mentions it is expected, but not required, you relocate into the school district. Do you sign your contract that day? What are the considerations?

_____

_____

_____

_____

5. Your team has just lost a close contest to a rival. The next morning's newspaper has quoted your star player as saying, "We were robbed; the officiating was horrible the entire game. They are not a better team than us, and I guarantee the outcome will be different the next time we play them." How do you handle this situation? Include how you will address the offending player, the story's author, and the opposing coach.

_____

_____

_____

_____

Practice Exercises

1. Find a partner for this assignment and disclose the sport you currently or most likely will coach. Prepare a list of fictitious interview questions for your partner, including pre-season, pre-game, and post-game questions. Purposefully include some questions that require a careful answer from the coach. Ask each other the questions while tape recording the interview session. Play back the session and critique each other's responses.

_____

_____

_____

_____

_____

_____

_____

_____

2. Prepare a statement describing your ideal relationship with the booster club and describing your ideal role in team fundraising. Include information provided in this chapter. Share your statements with a partner and critique each other's efforts.

_____

_____

_____

_____

_____

_____

_____

_____

References

Appenzeller, H. (1993). *Managing sports and risk management strategies.* Durham, NC: Carolina Academic Press.

Helitzer, M. (1999). *The dream job: $port$ publicity, promotion and marketing.* Athens, OH: University Sports Press.

Sabock, R.J., & Sabock, M.D. (2005). *Coaching: A realistic perspective* (8th ed.). Lanham, MD: Rowman & Littlefield Publishing Inc.

Developing the Team

SECTION 3

CHAPTER
11
Selecting the Squad

Selecting a team is one of the season's first duties. The process of cutting a player and then subsequently dealing with unhappy student-athletes and their parents is not a pleasant experience even for the most experienced coach.

This chapter provides the four basic principles of evaluating student-athletes and subsequently selecting a team. This chapter also identifies the appropriate measures to use when announcing cuts. The discussion questions also consider several points when selecting a team, including how the last roster spots are determined and what responsibility a coach has toward those students who did not make the team. The discussion questions and scenarios investigate whether a talented sophomore should play junior varsity or varsity and what to do when a returning player is injured before the tryouts. A practice exercise provides a coach an opportunity to make these difficult decisions.

Warm-Up

Here we introduce coaches to the basic principles used when evaluating or selecting a team. Coaches need to have a system in place when making these important decisions. We also offer insight on the appropriate way to cut student-athletes when faced with this difficult task.

1. Four basic principles of evaluating and selecting a team (Sabock & Sabock, 2005):
   a. Potential
   b. Desire and ability
      i. Desire to play, win, work hard, learn, get better, and compete
   c. Team priorities
   d. Ability to perform in game play
2. Appropriate methodology when cutting student-athletes:
   a. Personally notify each student-athlete whether he or she has made the squad.
   b. Post a list in a secure area and indicate times you are available to discuss your decisions when personally notifying each student-athlete is not feasible due to the high number of student-athletes who tried out for the team.
   c. Never announce the squad or those who did not make the squad at a team meeting or do anything else that increases the embarrassment the "cut" student-athletes are experiencing.

http://health.jbpub.com/book/prepare

Go to the web component of *Preparing the Successful Coach* at http://health.jbpub.com/book/prepare for web exercises and a suggested reading list.

Discussion Questions

1. a. Sabock and Sabock claim there are players who can, players who can't, and players with potential. How should a coach consider potential when selecting a squad?

_____

_____

b. How might your team's talent level affect this decision?

_____

_____

2. When selecting the last roster spots, should coaches look at filling certain positions or take the best athlete available (e.g., a left-handed pitcher, a backup kicker, a defensive specialist)?

_____

_____

_____

3. Is it automatic that a student-athlete on the team as a junior makes it as a senior? Why or why not?

_____

_____

_____

4. Is it automatic that student-athletes who were primary contributors on last year's team make this year's squad, especially in lieu of them having a poor tryout?

_____

_____

_____

5. What should coaches consider before selecting a senior they perceive would not play much?

_____

_____

_____

6. a. What should a coach do with the sophomore who would contribute to the varsity team as a role player but could gain more playing experience at the sophomore level?

_____

_____

_____

b. Should a coach consider the student-athlete's preference?

_____

_____

_____

c. What are the advantages and disadvantages to each possibility?

_____

_____

d. Should the student-athlete or his or her parents have any input in this decision? Why or why not?

_____

_____

e. Is it fair on a student-athlete's time to ask him or her to play for both teams?

_____

_____

7. How should a coach balance talent and attitude when selecting a team?

_____

_____

_____

8. How can a student-athlete's family's status in the community affect the selection process? A coach's relationship (neighbor, friend, etc.) with the student's family?

_____

_____

_____

9. Do coaches already have in their mind who will make the team and thus is the tryout merely a formality?

_____

_____

10. a. What are the primary and secondary purposes of hosting tryouts? Should a coach use a formal assessment tool when evaluating talent during tryouts?

_____

_____

b. How many cuts should be made? After how many practices should a first cut be made?

_____

_____

c. How should a coach notify student-athletes being cut?

_____

_____

_____

11. What are the positives and negatives of the practice where some student-athletes are named to the team while tryouts exist for the last few spots?

_____

_____

_____

_____

Scenarios

1. Your softball team has 16 varsity uniforms and your squad size cannot exceed that number. Jill was a reserve outfielder and pinch runner as a junior. She suffered severe injuries in a car accident last fall and will not be cleared to play until after the tryouts. Your current junior class is strong, and even if healthy Jill would likely not crack the starting lineup. You will have to cut a promising junior if you select Jill. Jill is well liked by her teammates and has been faithfully adhering to her rehabilitation schedule. Whom do you select and why?

_____

_____

_____

_____

2. You are considering two student-athletes for the final roster spot on your soccer team. The first player's father is on the school board and has a reputation for confronting coaches over playing time, a rare commodity for the last spot. You do not anticipate any problems with the parents of the second player. Whom do you select and why?

_____

_____

_____

_____

3. Rob is a transfer student who started for a rival team last year. He has struggled during tryouts and would not make the team based solely on that performance. However, you have seen what he is capable of doing in game situations. Does Rob make your roster? Why or why not?

_____

_____

_____

_____

Practice Exercise

1. You are a volleyball coach who is allowed to keep 15 girls on your varsity roster. Eleven of the choices are easy; the last four are proving more difficult. Below are short bios on the remaining eight student-athletes trying out for the team. Select four of them. Find a partner and articulate back and forth your reasons for picking the girls you did.

   a. Amy: A junior with solid athletic ability. She can play most positions on the court, making her versatility in practice an asset. She is a talented swimmer and that is the sport where she devotes most of her off-season work.

   _____

   _____

   _____

   _____

   _____

   _____

   _____

   b. Patty: A senior back row player and setter. Patty was on the squad last year and accepted her role as a bench player. You believe her greatest asset is she would give the team that needed enthusiasm still as a senior. You do not believe she is one of your 15 best players this year.

   _____

   _____

   _____

   _____

   _____

   _____

   _____

   c. Rhonda: A sophomore middle hitter. Rhonda would be your second-string middle hitter at the varsity level and you must decide if it is better for her to get a few rotations in varsity matches or play full-time at the sophomore level. You do not want to postpone this decision until mid-season and risk disrupting team chemistry.

   _____

   _____

   _____

   _____

   _____

   _____

   _____

d. Toya: A junior outside hitter. Toya is one of the team's better servers and could be used in that aspect in a crucial spot in a match. However, her all-around game is not one of the 15 best.

_____

_____

_____

_____

_____

e. Janet: A junior setter. Janet was the starting setter on the sophomore squad last year and you would have predicted she would have been your top backup to your senior all-conference performer this year. However, she was passed on the depth chart by another player and has sulked throughout the entire tryout, something her teammates have noticed as much as you. She has the talent to be next season's starting setter and is one of your 15 best players, but you are unsure how her attitude may impact team chemistry.

_____

_____

_____

_____

_____

f. Hannah: A junior front-row player. Hannah is a solid blocker at either the outside or middle positions and is competent offensively, but she needs some further work. Her back-row skills are poor and you can't foresee her ever being a major contributor to the varsity program.

_____

_____

_____

_____

g. Maria: A senior outside hitter. Maria has not played formal volleyball since her freshman year, but she is friends with some of the girls and decided to try out. She is a good athlete and fits in with the team chemistry, but you are hesitant to give a roster spot to a new senior who will not make an impact in varsity matches.

_____

_____

_____

_____

_____

_____

h. Isabell: A junior middle hitter. Isabell is 6-foot-3 and you talked her into playing at the sophomore level last year, envisioning her as a project because she had never played organized volleyball before. She did not play much last year at the sophomore level because of nagging injuries. Her footwork on her approach still needs work and she must get more aggressive, but she has the potential to become a defensive asset to your club by next year. You perceive she is out for the team just as "something to do" and that she has not yet developed a passion for volleyball.

_____

_____

_____

_____

_____

_____

_____

_____

References

Sabock, R.J., & Sabock, M.D. (2005). _Coaching: A realistic perspective_ (8th ed.). Lanham, MD: The Rowman and Littlefield Publishing Group, Inc.

CHAPTER 12

Coach–Player Relationships

The relationship between players and coaches is multifaceted and may be impacted by personalities, goals, and age. The relationships coaches build with their student-athletes is an important, and often overlooked, aspect of the job. Such relationships can offer personal and professional satisfaction and may impact the team's success. The discussion questions elaborate on the player–coach relationship.

The role of team captains is also discussed. The discussion questions ask whether captains are necessary and how they should be selected.

Three scenarios are presented. They include a situation involving a player who is about to become homeless, a player who is a best friend with one of your children, and a team voting someone as captain that you cannot approve. A practice exercise forces coaches to articulate multiple opinions on team captains.

Warm-Up

Coaches are introduced to ways they can improve communication with their student-athletes, specifically through team captains. Several potential duties of team captains are identified.

1. Duties of the team captain (Manos, 2000):
  a. Be the bridge between the coaching staff and the team.
  b. Serve as a leader, by example and by word.
  c. Prevent hazing of younger athletes.
  d. Lead the warm-up before practice and matches.
  e. Address grievances with the coaches.
  f. Assist in making decisions concerning meal locations and so on.

http://health.jbpub.com/book/prepare

Go to the web component of *Preparing the Successful Coach* at http://health.jbpub.com/book/prepare for web exercises and a suggested reading list.

Discussion Questions

1. How important is the relationship between the coaches and the players in regard to the overall success of the team? Why?

_____

_____

_____

_____

2. What are the components of a good player–coach relationship? A rocky one?

_____

_____

_____

_____

3. a. Can a respected coach be a friend? Can a respected coach be a jerk? Can a coach who is a friend command full respect?

_____

_____

b. What is the relationship between friendship and respect as it pertains to coach–player relationships?

_____

_____

_____

c. What is the difference between being respected and being liked?

_____

_____

_____

4. Coaches will have favorites. How difficult is it for a coach to play a student-athlete he or she dislikes over a favorite?

_____

_____

_____

_____

5. a. What crosses the line in a player–coach relationship away from the playing arena?

_____

_____

b. Should a coach spend time with a player away from the playing arena? Why or why not?

_____

_____

_____

© 2008 Jones and Bartlett Publishers, Inc.   www.jbpub.com

c. Should a coach take just one player on a scouting trip?

_____

_____

d. Can the existence of a line be a detriment to a coach's ability to be a role model, especially to student-athletes who otherwise have none?

_____

_____

_____

e. Is this line different if a coach's children are in high school? Why or why not?

_____

_____

_____

6. Do you agree with Manos' depiction of a captain's duties? Why or why not?

_____

_____

_____

_____

7. Are captains necessary? Why or why not?

_____

_____

_____

8. a. How may coaches use captains to improve their relationship with the entire team?

_____

_____

_____

b. Should the coach, the players, or a combination of both select captains?

_____

_____

_____

c. When should captains be selected?

_____

_____

_____

d. Must captains be seniors?

_____

_____

_____

e. What are some potential strengths and weaknesses of giving captains a lot of responsibility?

_____

_____

_____

9. a. When should a captain be replaced?

_____

_____

b. What if the captain suffers a season-ending injury early in the season?

_____

_____

_____

Scenarios

1. Michael is one of your star student-athletes. He comes from a broken home and does not have a solid home life; you are the most important adult figure in his life. Michael had been living with his mother, who recently moved in with a new boyfriend who does not want Michael tagging along. Michael has nowhere to go. You are considering taking him into your home. What are the considerations, both to Michael and the entire team?

_____

_____

_____

_____

2. You have always allowed your players to pick the team captains. This year the team picked Allison, a student-athlete with whom you have serious concerns over her ability to lead. You have had run-ins with Allison in the past and believe she is capable of rallying the team against you. The vote was 11–4 so it will be hard to overturn silently—the players will know what has happened. How do you handle this situation?

_____

_____

_____

3. Your son is the best friend of Jorge, one of your student-athletes. Your son asks whether Jorge can accompany the family during the upcoming weekend excursion to Indianapolis. You have allowed your son's older brother and sister to bring friends along on previous weekend vacations. What do you consider, and subsequently decide, concerning this request?

_____

_____

_____

_____

Practice Exercise

1. Write your opinions on the positives, negatives, role, and primary responsibilities of team captains. Also write a statement as to how you plan to use or not use captains on your team. Share your opinions with a colleague and ask each other questions accordingly.

_____

_____

_____

_____

_____

_____

_____

_____

Reference

Manos, K. (2000). Navigating with captains. *Athletic Management, 12*(2), 18–19.

The Star Athlete and the Third Stringer

Most coaches hope to someday have the opportunity to work with a star athlete. Coaching the star offers both rewards and challenges. Star athletes are sometimes portrayed as having a negative influence on a team. However, the strategies a coach can use to combat this negative influence and the positive opportunities that derive from having a star athlete are often overlooked.

Conversely, every coach will have the student-athletes who do not garner much playing time, the stereotypical "bench warmer." Coaching these athletes also offers both rewards and challenges. Sometimes coaches are guilty of overlooking these athletes' contribution to the team and taking advantage of their love for the team and the game.

This chapter reviews the relationship between a coach and both the star athletes and the third-string athletes. Information is provided on how to treat the third-string athlete, and the discussion questions ask if the star should be treated differently and be rested more during practices. The questions also ask when a star player should be removed from the team and focus on different ways a coach can use the bench.

Six scenarios offer prospective coaches situations relevant to the star or third-string athlete. These scenarios include a student-athlete injured throughout the week's practice but cleared for the game. Also included is a situation where a coach has to decide to call a crucial play for the star athlete, realizing this is what the opponent expects, or for a second option the opponent will less likely expect.

In this section we introduce coaches to another component of effectively improving communication with student-athletes. Strategies on how coaches can effectively communicate and interact with their third-string athletes are identified. Coaches often underestimate the role these individuals contribute to the team.

1. How to treat the third-string athlete:
   a. Never promise them playing time in a game you anticipate will be a blowout.
   b. When they are in the game, coach them with the same passion you would the first string.
   c. When they are in the game, demand the same bench behavior from the first string that you expect from the third string.
   d. Find ways throughout the season, both during games and practices, to implicitly and explicitly call positive attention to their contributions to the team's effort.

Discussion Questions

1. a. Do coaches knowingly treat the star athlete differently? If so, how? Should they? ✔

_____

_____

b. Do coaches who were once star athletes themselves have a better understanding of the pressures of being the star player? What are some examples of these pressures or responsibilities?

_____

_____

2. How much should coaches worry about how other players perceive whether the coach treats the star athlete differently? ✔

_____

_____

_____

_____

3. A team is as good as how hard their best players practice: agree or disagree? ✔

_____

_____

_____

_____

4. How do coaches expect their star athlete to lead the team? Are the stars always vocal leaders? What is meant when one is described as a "leader by example"? ✔

_____

_____

_____

_____

5. a. At what point should coaches cut their losses and kick the star player off the team if he or she is a bad apple? ✔

_____

_____

_____

b. What are the considerations, both in the program's short and long term?

_____

_____

_____

c. Does it matter if the team is winning or not?

_____

_____

_____

d. Does it matter if the other players like the star or not?

_____

_____

_____

e. Is there such a thing as an "irreplaceable" player?

_____

_____

_____

6. Should coaches be more careful with their stars in practice situations? If so, how? Should a coach let the "banged up" star rest more in practice but allot him or her regular playing time in the game? Why or why not?

_____

_____

_____

_____

7. Offensive strategies are often devised around star players. How much is too much?

_____

_____

_____

_____

8. Should coaches, in sports for which the following is applicable, give star athletes easier defensive assignments to maximize their energies on their offensive production? Why or why not?

_____

_____

_____

_____

9. How should coaches motivate the star athletes not being pushed by their teammates in practice?

_____

_____

_____

_____

10. Who is generally more jealous of the star, other players or parents?

_____

_____

_____

_____

11. Do you agree or disagree with the statements provided in the background information on how to treat the third-string athlete? Why or why not?

_____

_____

_____

12. How can coaches make third-string players believe they are an integral part of the team?

_____

_____

_____

13. a. What does a coach expect of third-string student-athletes?

_____

_____

b. How should a coach communicate these expectations, especially to the student-athlete who does not have the talent to realistically pass teammates on the depth chart?

_____

_____

14. Are "Hustle" or "Spirit" awards specifically geared toward third-string players rewarding or demeaning?

_____

_____

_____

15. What are the possible opportunities and threats with placing a less talented third-string player into a starting role for no other reason than to motivate the first-string players?

_____

_____

_____

16. Is there an amount of time remaining in the game where putting the third-stringers in the game is insulting? Why or why not?

_____

_____

_____

17. Should a coach attempt to place third-stringers in the game with first and second stringers? Is it insulting to "empty the bench"?

_____

_____

_____

_____

18. What are some ways a coach can arrange for a third-string athlete with an obvious mental or physical handicap to get involved in a contest?

_____

_____

_____

_____

19. Should a coach allow seniors to start on senior night if they otherwise would not? What are the considerations?

_____

_____

_____

_____

20. Coaches want student-athletes who understand their roles. Do coaches want them to accept it? What is the fine line?

_____

_____

_____

_____

21. Should coaches limit the practice opportunities of third-stringers in favor of more reps for the first string during pre-game warm-ups (number of swings, serves, shots, etc.)?

_____

_____

_____

22. Would it ever be appropriate to place third-stringers in a game situation that would humble them because they need to learn they are not as good as they think?

_____

_____

_____

_____

Scenarios

1. It is 3:35 and your star student-athlete is still not on the team bus that was scheduled to leave at 3:30. You do not know where he or she is. What do you do?

_____

_____

_____

2. Your star tailback was banged up in last week's game. He has not been able to practice all week, forcing the second- and third-string backs to get more repetitions in practice. These two student-athletes expect to get some carries in Friday's game. Your star is cleared just in time for Friday's contest. Who starts the game? Who gets the bulk of the carries? What are the considerations? The ramifications?

_____

_____

_____

3. Your high school softball team is not allowed to cut. Mandy is a student-athlete with little talent, skills, or athletic ability. Her performance level is so poor that it lessens the team's performance during any drill or simulation you attempt to instruct. How should this student-athlete be included (or not included) in practice?

_____

_____

4. Your high school association allows a basketball player to compete in 30 games, varsity and junior varsity combined. Shelton usually plays varsity, but you would like him to play one junior varsity game so he can log some extra playing minutes. This means he will have to sit out one varsity game. Your varsity team is experiencing a lopsided win. You will be able to get your third-string players in the game. This game would be a good opportunity to sit Shelton, but then he would be the only player who does not get in this game—a potentially embarrassing situation for him. What do you decide and why?

_____

_____

_____

5. Brian has mild cerebral palsy that impacts both his cognitive and psychomotor skills. Brian has been the manager for the football, basketball, and baseball teams for all four years of high school. The baseball season has 2 weeks left and some of the baseball players and members of the student body approach you as baseball coach. They would like Brian to dress one of the upcoming games and be used as a pinch-runner. They ideally would like for you to arrange with the opposing coach to allow him to steal a base. How do you approach this situation?

_____

_____

_____

6. Your basketball team has the ball and is trailing by one point with 12 seconds left when you call a time out to design your last play. Allison is your all-conference performer and you anticipate your opponent will double team her. Are you confident in Allison's ability to hit the shot while double teamed, exuding a "you win or lose with your best" philosophy, or do you design a play where Allison is a decoy and one of her teammates, likely to be open, is asked to step up and hit the winning shot? What are the considerations, both short term (this game) and long term?

_____

_____

_____

© 2008 Jones and Bartlett Publishers, Inc.   www.jbpub.com

Practice Exercise

1. Identify how you will communicate your expectations to your third-string athletes. Specifically, what points will you ensure to get across about their potential playing time, their role on the team, and expectations of them? What questions will you ask them? Share your thoughts with a colleague and critique each other's effort.

_____

_____

_____

_____

_____

_____

_____

_____

CHAPTER

14

The Starting Line-Up and the Bench

Pre-game introductions in some sports have made inclusion in the starting line-up a bigger deal than necessary. Substitution rules in other sports may impact the decision on who compiles the starting line-up and how to utilize the bench.

Coaches have many things to consider when deciding on a starting line-up. Suggestions are provided to aid the coach in these decisions. This chapter asks prospective coaches to consider several factors that enter into this decision. The discussion questions ask coaches if seniors should start ahead of juniors and whether the starting line-up should remain constant. The scenarios include a situation where a coach must decide who should comprise the starting line-up and a situation where a coach is faced with a decision concerning changing the starting line-up.

Coaches also have several considerations when deciding how to best use their bench. The discussion questions ask coaches to consider whether match-ups dictate how to use their bench and how to determine whether certain student-athletes are better accustomed to come off the bench.

Warm-Up

In this section we introduce coaches to strategies concerning two important topics. First, we offers considerations for coaches to use when determining the starting line-up, something that can be important but also can be overemphasized. Second, we offer suggestions to coaches on how to best utilize the bench.

1. Considerations when determining the starting line-up:
   a. Consistency from game to game
   b. Match-ups
   c. Chemistry
   d. Who is more or less comfortable off the bench
   e. Substitution rules

2. Considerations for utilizing the bench:
   a. Match-ups
   b. Substitution rules
   c. Consistent roles
   d. How the starting line-up is performing
   e. Number of games in upcoming days

http://health.jbpub.com/book/prepare

Go to the web component of *Preparing the Successful Coach* at http://health.jbpub.com/book/prepare for web exercises and a suggested reading list.

Discussion Questions

1. Do student-athletes believe starting is a big deal? From where does this attitude stem?

_____

_____

_____

_____

2. What must a coach consider when determining the starting line-up? Should it always necessarily be the best players? Why or why not?

_____

_____

_____

_____

3. Should seniors start ahead of juniors who are comparable in ability? What are the considerations? How might it depend on the talent of the sophomore class?

_____

_____

_____

_____

4. a. What is the difference in mental preparation between starting and coming off the bench?

_____

_____

b. Are some players better accustomed to one or the other? How can coaches determine this?

_____

_____

5. a. Should a coach avoid juggling the starting line-up? Why or why not?

_____

_____

b. What are the advantages and disadvantages in a practice when the starting line-up for the next game is always predetermined?

_____

_____

_____

6. a. Should a coach have a set philosophy concerning use of the bench or should he or she adjust to the talent level?

_____

_____

_____

b. What are the advantages and disadvantages of having a deep bench?

_____

_____

_____

7. Should bench players have a consistent role from game to game? Why or why not?

_____

_____

_____

_____

8. a. Do match-ups affect both the starting line-up and utilization of the bench?

_____

_____

_____

b. Do student-athletes fully comprehend this, especially when it means a limited role in the next game despite a good performance in the previous one?

_____

_____

_____

9. What are the advantages and disadvantages to specializing student-athletes for specific roles (defensive specialist, left-handed reliever)? At what level should coaches start specializing student-athletes?

_____

_____

_____

10. a. What are the considerations when making the line-up for individual sports such as wrestling, tennis, and golf?

_____

_____

b. How much should a coach balance head-to-head competition in practice against how both student-athletes perform in varsity match play?

_____

_____

_____

Scenarios

1. Your soccer team had a 2–3 record when your goalie suffered an injury. The team went 3–1 with the backup goalie in net. You still believe the original starter is a better goalie, but the team played with more confidence with the second-stringer. The original starter has been cleared to play in tomorrow's game. Who starts and both how and when do you inform both student-athletes of your decision?

_____

_____

_____

2. Mandy and Diana have alternated as your left-fielder. Both players are comparable defensively. Mandy has been on a hot streak and has subsequently earned more starts recently; she is batting 7 for 14 in her last six games and is having quality at-bats. However, today's opposing pitcher has an overpowering fast ball and traditionally Diana has a quicker bat and has better at-bats in such match-ups. Which player starts in left field today?

_____

_____

_____

3. Shontel and Byron have battled all training camp for the starting quarterback position. Shontel is a senior who was the second-string quarterback last year. He has performed slightly better than Byron, who is a junior, during training camp. Your coaching staff unanimously believes next year's team has a chance to be special, and you are tempted to start Byron so he can gain valuable experience in preparation for next season. Whom do you start and why?

_____

_____

_____

4. Butch and Jermaine have battled all season for the top spot at one of your weight classes. Butch is in 8–3 in his matches, whereas Jermaine is 2–4. However, Jermaine has consistently outperformed Butch during the past 2 weeks of practice. Who gets the nod in the upcoming invitational and why?

_____

_____

_____

Practice Exercise

1. Identify the qualities of a student-athlete you want in the starting line-up. What other qualities, besides obviously talent, will be deciding factors in your decision? How will these other qualities compare with talent when making your final decisions? Share your thoughts with a colleague and critique each other's effort.

_____

_____

_____

_____

_____

_____

_____

© 2008 Jones and Bartlett Publishers, Inc.   www.jbpub.com

EXERCISE 14.0

CHAPTER 15

The Multiple-Sport Athlete and Coach

High school athletes often participate in multiple sports, and high school coaches often have dual coaching responsibilities. The overlapping seasons and summer expectations can create conflicts.

This chapter looks at the challenges for the coach in both dealing with the multiple-sport athlete and handling his or her own dual assignments. This chapter also provides information concerning the growing trend, especially in larger high schools, of student-athletes specializing in one sport and offers tips to those who coach two sports. The discussion questions offer insight into possible conflicts and pressures student-athletes and coaches may encounter and stress the importance of communication. These possible conflicts include the balancing of two sports while one is in season and another has begun their preseason and the numbers of days off student-athletes are allowed between seasons.

The scenarios are realistic situations that allow coaches to look at the balance necessary when coaching multiple-sport athletes or when coaching two sports. A practice exercise forces the coach to articulate his or her philosophy on multiple-sport athletes.

Warm-Up

Here we introduce coaches to the advantages, disadvantages, and cautions pertaining to student-athletes who specialize in one sport. We also offer suggestions to the coach who coaches more than one sport to ensure he or she can offer all of his or her student-athletes an equitable experience.

1. Advantages and disadvantages to sport specialization (Stankovich, 2006):
   a. Advantages
      i. Potentially greater exposure to college coaches
      ii. More competitions in the primary sport of emphasis
      iii. More opportunities to review and refine athletic skills
   b. Disadvantages
      i. Increase risk for burnout or withdrawal
      ii. Missing opportunities to learn new skills, meet new teammates, and have different life experiences

2. Arguments against sport specialization (Susanji & Stewart, n.d.):
   a. May conflict with school mission with goals to provide student-athletes potential for greatest personal growth.
   b. Research suggests multi-sport athletes earn better grades.

c. Exposure to different coaching styles and values allow student-athlete the opportunity to grow into a well-rounded athlete.

   d. Student-athlete's gain the opportunity to learn transferable athletic skills.

   e. Research refutes the notion specialization makes one better at their primary sport.

3. Tips for the multiple-sport coach:

   a. Make your in-season sport your priority, regardless of whether it is your preference.

   b. Do not allow the student-athletes in your "second" sport to feel slighted.

   c. Do not alter the practice times of your in-season sport to accommodate the practice schedule of your pre-season sport.

   d. Balance your summer obligations to both teams as reasonably as possible.

   e. Lean more on your assistant coaches and captains during the off-season or pre-season while you are in-season with your second sport.

   f. Communicate your expectations with your administration and coaching staffs about the conflicts that inevitably will surface coaching two sports.

---

http://health.jbpub.com/book/prepare

Go to the web component of *Preparing the Successful Coach* at http://health.jbpub.com/book/prepare for web exercises and a suggested reading list.

Discussion Questions

1. Critique the tips for the multiple-sport coach. With which do you agree and disagree? Why?

_____

_____

_____

2. a. Should high school coaches have the authority to tell their student-athletes they cannot play other sports?

_____

_____

b. What tactics do some coaches use to imply this without directly saying it? Are such pressure tactics truly different from blatantly disallowing it? Why or why not?

_____

_____

_____

c. Are such tactics ethical? Why or why not?

_____

_____

_____

d. What recourse should student-athletes or fellow coaches have available to them when one coach is applying such pressure? When and how should the athletic director become involved?

_____

_____

_____

3. a. Describe the balance of expectations for a two-sport student-athlete playing for one team that is in season and a second team that is in pre-season.

_____

_____

b. What crosses the line of devoting too much time to the pre-season sport? Does it matter if the student-athlete is a bench player in his or her current sport and a contributor in the pre-season sport? Does it matter if a student-athlete has a favorite?

_____

_____

c. What is fair for the in-season coach to expect from this student-athlete? The pre-season coach?

_____

_____

d. Should the pre-season coach be expected to ask permission from the in-season coach to allow the student-athletes to practice? What is an appropriate response from the in-season coach if asked?

_____

_____

e. Should an athletic department policy be in place to handle such matters, or should it be left for individual coaches to work out?

_____

_____

4. How might the answers to the above questions change if the second sport is a club or other non-scholastic sport?

_____

_____

_____

5. a. Does a returning starter automatically get his or her position back if he or she missed pre-season practice playing another sport?

_____

_____

b. What are the ramifications of each answer?

_____

_____

_____

c. Should an athlete be told his or her participation in another sport, and thus missing practices, gives teammates an opportunity to take his or her spot?

_____

_____

6. a. How difficult is it for two-sport coaches to deal with student-athletes who play both sports for them but end the first sport in the doghouse?

_____

_____

b. Would coaches be justified in disallowing a student-athlete to try out for a second sport they coach because of issues encountered in the first sport? Why or why not?

_____

_____

_____

c. How difficult would it be for players not to hold grudges?

_____

_____

_____

7. What are the considerations for allowing student-athletes to play two sports in the same season (such as football and soccer *or* softball and track and field)?

_____

_____

_____

_____

8. What problems may multi-sport athletes encounter in the summer? What can coaches do to alleviate these conflicts?

_____

_____

_____

9. How many days off should a coach allow a student-athlete who just finished one sport before he or she begins practicing in the second? How many days off should a coach be allowed?

_____

_____

_____

10. a. What should be expected from a two-sport coach in the off-season of one sport while his or her second sport is in-season? Does it matter if the coach is an assistant in the in-season sport and a head coach in the off-season sport? Vice versa?

_____

_____

_____

b. How should two-sport coaches be expected to balance their duties in the summer?

_____

_____

11. How difficult is it for a two-sport coach to not indirectly reveal to players he or she has a favorite sport? How much are student-athletes concerned with this?

_____

_____

_____

12. Review these discussion questions again. How important is communication to all of them? How many of these potential situations are likely to be diffused with good communication?

_____

_____

_____

_____

Scenarios

1. You are a head basketball coach at your school. You have a policy mandating a one-game suspension for each game a student-athlete misses. Your school's volleyball team advanced to the state tournament, held the same weekend as your Tip-Off Tournament. Two of your student-athletes are members of the volleyball team. Do you suspend them for each game missed, as your policy dictates, or do you make an exception? What are the ramifications of either decision?

_____

_____

_____

2. You are a coach of a fall sport suffering through a poor season. There are 2 weeks left in the season. Three of your student-athletes ask permission to attend pre-season basketball practice on alternate nights with your practices. You perceive they will quit your team if you do not go along with their request. What do you decide?

_____

_____

_____

3. You are a head swimming coach at your school and your team is in season. You arrive at school one morning and discover Tia, one of your swimmers, taking batting practice with other softball players. You have not forbidden such an action, but you ask her why she is in the cage. She tells you the softball coach expects her to start hitting and throwing. What should you tell Tia? How should you approach the softball coach?

_____

_____

_____

4. You are the wrestling and girl's soccer coach at your school. Wrestling is overwhelmingly your favorite sport. Your soccer pre-season begins while wrestling season still has 2 weeks left. You do not have an assistant coach for either sport. How should you balance these duties? What message do you send if you expect the girl's soccer team to wait to begin practice until wrestling season ends? What if the situation was reversed and soccer was your sport of choice? Would it be fair to shorten wrestling practices so you have more time to spend with the soccer athletes?

_____

_____

_____

5. You are an assistant football coach and head girl's soccer coach at your school. Girl's soccer is played in the spring and football is a fall sport. Football players not participating in a spring sport begin off-season weight lifting sessions at 6:00 A.M. You are the coach with the least seniority on the football staff and the head coach would like for you to be the one to arrive on campus to open the weight room. You have soccer practices or games daily after school and you believe opening and supervising the weight room makes for an unnecessarily long day. There are other coaches on the football staff who are not coaching a second sport. How do you approach this situation? How much does it depend on your desire to be a head football coach someday?

_____

_____

_____

6. Patrick is the starting midfielder on your soccer team. He informs you after the first week of practice the football coaches have approached him and inquired about his willingness to be the team's kicker. The football staff only expects him to be at games, and there are no conflicts with the soccer game schedule. There may be some away football games where the departure time necessitates missing soccer practice. You have two initial reactions: you are irritated the football coaches did not come to you first with this proposal, and you do not believe playing a second sport justifies missing practice. How do you respond and subsequently handle this situation?

_____

_____

_____

Practice Exercise

1. Write a half-page articulation on your philosophy toward multi-sport athletes. Include how you are or are not willing to accommodate them. Share your thoughts with a colleague and ask each other questions on your philosophies.

_____

_____

_____

_____

_____

_____

_____

_____

References

Stankovich, C. (2006, August). Sport specialization in high school sports: The pros and the cons. *Columbus Parent Magazine.* Retrieved August 2, 2006 from http://www.columbusparent.com/?story=columbusparent/march/sportsdoc.html.

Susanji, D., & Stewart, C. (n.d.). Specialization in sport: How early, how necessary? *Coaches' Information Service: Sport Science Information for Coaches.* Retrieved August 2, 2006 from http://coachesinfo.com/article/7/.

CHAPTER

16
Goals

Different coaches, administrators, and theorists offer multiple opinions on the value of setting goals. Goals can be qualitative or quantitative, ego oriented or task oriented (Zahariadis & Biddle, 2000), stated or unstated, and worthwhile or worthless. Coaches should have goals for the team and goals for different individuals; this process may be different in both individual and team sports. The coach has the responsibility to balance the individual goals for each squad member and the aspirations of the entire team. Coaches also have the responsibility to set clear and reasonable goals for themselves and their staff.

This chapter provides background material on setting goals. This includes categories of goals and examples of conflicting and complementary goals. The discussion questions include whether or not to have team goals and how to decide on accomplishable and worthwhile goals. The questions also inquire how goals may be different for individual sports.

Two separate scenarios ask coaches to help set goals for a team and individual sport. Two practice exercises afford coaches the opportunity to create goals for a fictitious team and for themselves.

Warm-Up

In this section coaches are introduced to multiple aspects of goal setting. The first two listings provide coaches with the components of setting goals and categories of different goals. These listings are followed by the SMART goal-setting approach. The final piece offers suggestions on how coaches can balance the setting and creation of goals between the student-athlete and the coach.

1. Components of setting goals:
  a. Identify opportunities
  b. Identify strengths
  c. Identify constraints
2. Categories of goals (Chelladurai, 2005; Frank, 2006; Zahariadis & Biddle, 2000):
  a. Official or formal stated goals: vague and general
    i. Example: "Play as hard as we can." *or* "Be competitive."
  b. Real goals: more specific
    i. Example: "Hold the opponent's shooting percentage below 43 percent for the season."
  c. Complementary: two goals that work together
    i. Example: "Hold the opponent's shooting percentage below 43 percent for the season *and* be in the top half of the league defensively in fewest points allowed."

d. Conflicting: two goals that do not work together
    i. Example: "Have two student-athletes advance to the state track meet during the sectional meet *and* finish first or second in the team scores at the sectional meet." Placing student-athletes in certain events where they will likely advance to state may hinder the maximum total points the team can achieve.
  e. Ego oriented: goals positively and highly correlated with status/recognition motives and negatively associated with team atmosphere motives
  f. Task oriented: goals positively and highly correlated with team atmosphere motives and skill development and negatively associated with status and recognition

3. SMART goal setting (Hurley, 2006):
  a. Specific (e.g., improve free throw percentage by 10%)
  b. Measurable (e.g., take 100 extra ground balls a week)
  c. Adjustable (e.g., due to an injury)
  d. Realistic (e.g., going from 3 to 20 to a state title)
  e. Time-based (e.g., short-term and long-term dates)

4. Balancing the creation of goals between student-athlete and coach (Thompson, 1995):
  a. Student-athletes will work toward excellence at a goal they created, as opposed to working hard to satisfy someone else when the goal is imposed on them.
  b. Ideally, student-athletes should work to develop their own goals; the coach should assist in the process.
  c. Some student-athletes simply have not developed the responsibility or ability to set their own goals. Suggestions may help these players.

---

http://health.jbpub.com/book/prepare

Go to the web component of *Preparing the Successful Coach* at http://health.jbpub.com/book/prepare for web exercises and a suggested reading list.

Discussion Questions

1. What are examples of qualitative and quantitative goals?

_____

_____

_____

2. What are examples of short-term and long-term goals?

_____

_____

_____

3. What are examples of ego-oriented and task-oriented goals?

_____

_____

_____

4. What are further examples of complementary and conflicting goals?

_____

_____

_____

5. Should a coach have more of one type of goals over another? Does it depend on how good the team is expected to be?

_____

_____

_____

_____

6. What are the considerations for determining team goals? Individual goals?

_____

_____

_____

_____

7. a. What are the problems with setting goals too high or too low?

_____

_____

_____

b. When should goals be rewritten during the middle of the season because the goals have proven to be too easy or too difficult?

_____

_____

_____

8. What are the differences in goals for athletes in team sports and individual sports?

_____

_____

_____

9. a. How often should progress toward goals be measured? Every game? Once a week? Only at the end of the season?

_____

_____

_____

_____

b. Identify specific examples of goals that can be measured during every game. Every practice. Use multiple sports.

_____

_____

_____

_____

10. How can some players' individual goals be detrimental to the team? What should a coach do to minimize this?

_____

_____

_____

_____

11. Do you agree with Thompson's assertion that student-athletes should have the primary role in goal development? Why or why not?

_____

_____

_____

_____

12. Does the community have their own set of goals for a team? What difficulties can this cause?

_____

_____

_____

_____

13. How much should a team's goals be made public?

_____

_____

_____

_____

14. How should coaches determine their own professional goals? Their goals for the assistant coaches? What are some examples of such goals?

_____

_____

_____

_____

Scenarios

1. Your team returns approximately 70% of its key players and statistical production from last season's state championship team. You believe this year's team is capable of repeating. You are also aware the post-season is a single elimination format. How would you set the goals for this team?

_____

_____

_____

_____

2. Marcos is one of your wrestlers and he has asked your assistance in setting his individual goals. Last year Marcos enjoyed a 22–13 record and placed fourth in the conference in his weight class. The conference champion and runner-up have graduated. How will you advise him?

_____

_____

_____

3. Your basketball program has quantitative goals for each game in the following categories: team field goal percentage, team free throw percentage, opponent's field goal percentage, rebound margin, and assist-to-turnover ratio. You did not meet any of these goals in last night's upset victory against one of your conference's top teams. Your players are more excited about their big victory than not meeting any of the targets. How do you handle this during the next practice?

_____

_____

_____

_____

Practice Exercises

1. You have recently been named the head coach for a sport of your choice at a school where the program has been a second-division team for the past 13 seasons. Participation numbers wane because of the team's reputation as a losing program. Identify both three short-term and long-term goals for the program. They can be quantitative and/or qualitative. Share these goals with a colleague and ask each other questions surrounding your work.

_____

_____

_____

_____

_____

_____

_____

_____

2. What are your professional goals? How do you plan on achieving them? How will you measure them? Draft such a document and articulate it to a colleague.

_____

_____

_____

_____

_____

_____

_____

_____

_____

References

Chelladurai, P. (2005). *Managing organizations for sport and physical activity* (2nd ed.). Scottsdale, AZ: Holcomb Hathaway Publishers.

Frank, M.A. (2006). *Using sport psychology skills to improve martial arts training: Setting goals to maximize performance.* Retrieved November 9, 2006 from http://www.behavioralconsultants.com/setting_goals.htm.

Hurley, K. (2006, November). *Healthy head games: Lessons for coaches and athletes.* Paper presented at the Illinois Association for Health, Physical Education, Recreation and Dance State Convention, St. Charles, IL.

Thompson, J. (1995). *Positive coaching: Building character and self-esteem through sports.* Portola Valley, CA: Warde Publishers.

Zahariadis, P.N., & Biddle, S.J. (2000, February). Goal orientations and participation motives in physical education and sport: Their relationship in English schoolchildren. *Athletic Insight: The Online Journal of Sport Psychology, 2*(1). Retrieved from http://www.athleticinsight.com/Vol2Iss1/English_Children.htm.

CHAPTER 17

Team Rules and Consequences

Most coaches have rules for their student-athletes. Coaches have different philosophies on the number of rules to have, the types of on- and off-court behavior to regulate, consequences for breaking rules, and how much effort should be placed on catching players breaking the rules.

Coaches also have the subsequent responsibility for enforcing the rules. Delivering consequences, equitably and without exception, can be challenging in several situations. The coach's ability to do so, however, can positively reflect on the program in the long term.

This chapter reviews the considerations of creating and enforcing rules. The purposes and categories of rules are provided. The discussion questions offer multiple considerations of team rules and consequences. These include how a coach's rules should coincide with an athletic department's code of conduct and the input student-athletes should have in determining rules and consequences. The questions also ask whether punishments should be clearly delineated or if coaches should be able to use their discretion.

Seven scenarios are presented, four of which include situations where a student misses a practice or game. A practice exercise allows prospective coaches to begin deriving some of their own team rules.

Warm-Up

Here coaches are introduced to the purposes of team rules. These purposes are then followed by a compilation of possible categories of team rules. The list is created from both actual rules coaches enforce and coaching literature.

1. Purposes of team rules (Hoch, 2003):
   a. Ensure appropriate behavior of student-athletes.
   b. Provide guidelines for sportsmanship and fair play.
   c. Articulate the concept student-athletes are ambassadors and role models.
   d. Delineate responsibilities athletes have to their team.

2. Possible categories of rules (D'Alfonso, 2001; Hoch, 2003; Workman, 2005):
   a. Players' language
   b. Interaction with officials, opponents, and coaches
   c. Players' dress when practicing, competing, or traveling
   d. Safety
   e. Curfew
   f. Use of alcohol, tobacco products, illicit drugs, and supplements
   g. Attendance at practice

h. Family vacation policies
i. Transportation policies
j. Cell phone usage

http://health.jbpub.com/book/prepare

Go to the web component of *Preparing the Successful Coach* at http://health.jbpub.com/book/prepare for web exercises and a suggested reading list.

Discussion Questions

1. What are some examples of team rules?

_____

_____

_____

_____

2. a. What are the advantages and disadvantages of having written formalized rules?

_____

_____

_____

b. Should a coach have student-athletes formally sign a document indicating they have received the rules? Have parents sign?

_____

_____

_____

_____

c. How many rules are too many?

_____

_____

_____

3. A coach cannot have a rule for everything. Should there be a general understanding or a specific rule indicating that student-athletes should always behave in a manner representing the team? Why or why not?

_____

_____

_____

_____

4. a. Is it better to have cut-and-dried consequences for breaking specific rules or leave punishment to be determined by the situation?

_____

_____

_____

b. What are the advantages and disadvantages of both?

_____

_____

_____

c. Does the degree of behavior matter (e.g., one beer vs. intoxication)?

_____

_____

d. Does the reason for the behavior matter (e.g., self-defense in a fight)?

_____

_____

e. Should a punishment be reduced when a student admits his or her wrongdoing? What factors should be considered for such an admission?

_____

_____

5. Some athletic departments may have codes of conduct for which all student-athletes must abide. These codes may include specific rules and consequences. Should a coach have the freedom to enforce tougher consequences than the school's code of conduct? Why or why not?

_____

_____

_____

6. a. What are the differences between a coach proactively enforcing the rules and a coach exuding a "don't get caught" mentality?

_____

_____

b. Describe the fine line between a coach proactively enforcing the rules and not trusting his or her student-athletes.

_____

_____

7. a. How should a coach handle a situation in which he or she learns of an alleged rules violation through a second-hand source?

_____

_____

b. What if the source is a parent?

_____

_____

_____

c. What if the source is one of your players who did not witness the alleged rules violation first-hand?

_____

_____

_____

8. a. What are legitimate reasons for being late or absent from a practice? A game? A team function?

_____

_____

_____

b. How should the following situations be handled?
  i. Family vacations?

_____

_____

_____

  ii. Academic field trips?

_____

_____

_____

  iii. College visits?

_____

_____

_____

  iv. Doctor or dental visits?

_____

_____

_____

c. Should the decision to suspend student-athletes for missing games due to family vacations, academic field trips, college visits, or doctor visits be left up to individual coaches or should a policy exist for the entire athletic department? What are the advantages and disadvantages of both?

_____

_____

_____

9. Should rules apply to the off-season? Why or why not?

_____

_____

_____

10. Should rules apply to incoming freshmen the summer after their eighth grade year? Why or why not?

_____

_____

_____

11. a. How much say should student-athletes have in making their own rules? Their punishments?

_____

_____

b. Should players ever be given the opportunity to vote a teammate off the team? Why or why not?

_____

_____

12. Should a coach have rules governing a player's personal appearance away from the playing arena (i.e., facial hair, tattoos, body piercing, appropriate dress)? Why or why not?

_____

_____

_____

13. Does a student-athlete deserve due process before a consequence is levied?

_____

_____

_____

14. How difficult is it for a coach to not hold a grudge against a student-athlete who has broken a rule but who faithfully served the punishment?

_____

_____

_____

Scenarios

1. You and a friend enter the local pizza establishment. You discover four of your players sitting in a booth being obnoxious and treating their waitress and other patrons rudely. These student-athletes are technically not breaking any rules, but their behavior is inappropriate. What should you do?

_____

_____

_____

2. One of your starters missed the team bus. She arrives at the game just before the start with her parents, who drove her 45 minutes to get there. She has no legitimate excuse for being late, but now expects to be in the starting line-up. You did not have a stated consequence for such an action. What do you do?

_____

_____

_____

3. One of your players is traveling with her parents to visit family during the Christmas break. She and her parents informed you of this before the season started. She will miss no games but will miss two practices. Your team rules state a player must sit out a game for each practice they miss. What do you do? What are the ramifications?

_____

_____

_____

_____

4. Jennifer, the anchor of two of your swimming relays, was caught breaking a rule that warrants a one-meet suspension. The next meet happens to be the conference championship. Jennifer has accepted her penalty gracefully, but the other three members of the relay team come to you before the bus leaves. They believe punishing Jennifer also unfairly punishes them because their chance to win conference is adversely affected without their best swimmer in the relay. How do you respond?

_____

_____

_____

_____

5. Julie is a member of the softball team and is a talented volleyball player. Several NCAA Division II schools are recruiting her and one such school has invited her to attend a tryout. Julie will have to miss Saturday's softball doubleheader to attend the tryout. How should you handle this?

_____

_____

_____

_____

6. Charles, your returning starting offensive lineman, had to miss the first three games of the season serving a suspension resulting from a second violation of the school's code of conduct. Charles worked hard at practice each day during his suspension, supported his teammates at the games, and in your opinion has dutifully "served his time." Charles' blocking ability is a big part of your running game, and his performance has been missed. You plan on starting him the first series this weekend because both his punishment is over and the team needs him. Your assistant coaches agree Charles is one of the team's five best offensive linemen but believe the wrong message is being sent in allowing someone who let the team down to regain his starting role so quickly. What do you do?

_____

_____

_____

7. One of your soccer player's parents calls you on Sunday afternoon. They inform you of a party they learned about from their son where allegedly several of your players were breaking the team's alcohol policy. How do you proceed?

_____

_____

_____

_____

Practice Exercise

1. Create three off-the-field and three on-the-field rules you would have for your team. Then decide how you would determine the consequences for student-athletes who break these rules. Share these rules with a colleague and ask each other questions surrounding your team rules.

_____

_____

_____

_____

_____

_____

_____

References

D'Alfonso, K. (2001). *Lady Raiders' basketball rules 2000–2001* [Brochure]. East Peoria, IL: Author.

Hoch, D. (2003). Considerations for developing team rules. *Strategies, 16*(4), 29–30.

Workman, J. (2005). *Tremont Junior/Senior High School Turks parent/coach communication* [Brochure]. Tremont, IL: Author.

EXERCISE 17.0

Team
Psychology

CHAPTER

18

Motivation

Coaches have student-athletes who are motivated to perform or excel in several different ways. A coach's personality and philosophy may impact how he or she attempts to motivate the team. Motivation is more than the fiery pre-game speech that makes for great entertainment. This chapter reviews the different motivation tactics and addresses the coach's role in motivating student-athletes.

This chapter outlines the characteristics of a coach who is a good motivator, challenges established motivational techniques, and asks what the coach's role is to motivate student-athletes. The existing literature on motivation is reviewed, including the definitions of motivation, intrinsic motivation, extrinsic motivation, optimal arousal, and locus of control. Strategies are included that increase optimal arousal and effectively motivate student-athletes. The discussion questions ask coaches how and whether they should use different styles to motivate different student-athletes, to critique the effectiveness of varying threats and incentives as motivational tools, and to assess the value of swearing as a motivational tactic.

Three scenarios are presented, including one that asks coaches to determine how to best motivate a lethargic team and a second where coaches may need to review their motivational techniques. Two practice exercises ask coaches to critique a quote from the literature on motivation and to identify what motivates them to continue coaching.

Warm-Up

In this section coaches are introduced to the definitions of motivation, intrinsic motivation, extrinsic motivation, and optimal arousal. This section also discusses best practices for coaches when motivating their student-athletes and when attempting to enhance their intrinsic motivation.

1. Definition of motivation: A condition within an individual that initiates activity directed toward a goal

2. Intrinsic and extrinsic motivation (Frank, 2002; Jensen & Overman, 2003; Wuest & Bucher, 2006):
   a. Intrinsic: internal in nature
      i. Desire to develop one's body or physique
      ii. Desire to have fun
      iii. Desire to test one's limits
      iv. Ego reinforcement, stemming from a feeling of conquest
      v. Emotional fulfillment upon accomplishing a goal
      vi. The ability of an individual to self-motivate by setting goals
      vii. Leads to greater consistency in performance without the instructor's presence

b. Extrinsic: external in nature
  i. Desire to win awards, championships, or recognition
  ii. Desire to have material proof of achievement
  iii. Desire to appease and to receive recognition from parents, coaches, or the community at-large
  iv. The reliance on an outside source to perform

3. How coaches can enhance intrinsic motivation in their student-athletes (Frank, 2002):
  a. Offer higher level of praise and encouragement
  b. Offer informational feedback
  c. Minimize punishment-oriented feedback to female athletes

4. Six keys for motivating athletes (Kohl, n.d.):
  a. Teach athletes how to perform their skills.
  b. Refuse to accept poor performance as "the best they can do."
  c. Recognize and glorify productive effort.
  d. Provide positive reinforcement extensively to all the players.
  e. Build a personal relationship with each student-athlete.
  f. Listen and gather information before offering advice; do not separate the respect for the task from the athlete's point of view.

5. Components to effectively motivate young athletes (Lenti, 1996):
  a. Build the coach-athlete relationship
    i. Coaches must realize they are coaching people, not machines.
    ii. Coaches should demonstrate an interest in all facets of a student-athlete's life.
  b. Develop a winning attitude
    i. Use goal-setting for teams and individuals.
    ii. Adjust goals if necessary so athletes have a sense of achievement, motivating them to work harder.
  c. Provide incentives
  d. Do not motivate by fear

6. Definition of optimal arousal and strategies to help your athletes experience it (Martens, 2004):
  a. The level of arousal is not too low where one is bored and not too high where one is fearful or anxious; it varies from person to person.
  b. Coaches can help athletes experience optimal arousal through the following strategies:
    i. Fit the difficulty of the skills to be learned to the student-athlete's ability.
    ii. Use a wide variety of drills and activities to practice skills.
    iii. Keep everyone active as opposed to standing around waiting their turn.
    iv. Avoid constant instruction during practices and games.
    v. Do not constantly evaluate athletes while a game is in progress.

7. Locus of control and the locus of control scale (Brown, 1999):
  a. Locus of control is the degree to which individuals believe their lives are controlled by internal or external factors.
  b. The locus of control scale consists of three components:
    i. I—*Internal* is the extent to which one believes his or her life and actions are controlled by internal factors.
    ii. P—*Powerful others* is the extent to which one believes his or her life and actions are controlled by powerful others.
    iii. C—*Chance* is the extent to which one believes his or her life and actions are controlled by chance.

http://health.jbpub.com/book/prepare

Go to the web component of *Preparing the Successful Coach* at http://health.jbpub.com/book/prepare for web exercises and a suggested reading list.

Discussion Questions

1. What are the characteristics of a coach who is a good motivator? A poor motivator?

_____

_____

_____

_____

2. What are effective motivational tactics? Ineffective motivational tactics?

_____

_____

_____

3. a. How successful are threats (running, playing time, practice going late) as motivational tools?

_____

_____

b. Are these better for short-term or long-term motivation?

_____

_____

c. Can a coach overuse such threats?

_____

_____

4. a. How successful are incentives (shorter practices, exclusion from a drill, tangible items such as stickers) as motivational tools?

_____

_____

b. Are these better for short-term or long-term motivation?

_____

_____

c. Can a coach overuse such incentives?

_____

_____

5. Critique Kohl's six keys to motivate athletes and Lenti's components to effectively motivate student-athletes. With which do you agree and with which do you disagree? Why?

_____

_____

_____

6. Critique Martens' strategies to help student-athletes experience optimal arousal.

_____

_____

_____

_____

7. Should coaches use different tactics to motivate different players? Why or why not? What are the ramifications of each answer?

_____

_____

_____

_____

8. a. Does a coach have a responsibility to motivate his or her student-athletes?

_____

_____

_____

b. Describe how this responsibility should be balanced between the coach and the student-athlete.

_____

_____

_____

c. Who else, if anyone, has a role in motivating the student-athlete?

_____

_____

_____

9. a. Can a coach be a successful motivator without raising his or her voice? Explain.

_____

_____

b. Coaches who are not "yellers and screamers" have been criticized for not being passionate and thus not able to motivate their student-athletes. Is such criticism fair? Why or why not?

_____

_____

_____

10. How successful is swearing as a motivational technique?

_____

_____

_____

a. Does its use as a motivating tool outweigh its inappropriateness?

_____

_____

_____

b. Can swearing be effective if used sparingly?

_____

_____

c. What words cross the line under any circumstance?

_____

_____

11. a. Does a coach receiving technical fouls, yellow cards, and so on motivate student-athletes? Why or why not?

_____

_____

_____

b. Does its use as a motivational tool outweigh its inappropriateness?

_____

_____

c. Does receiving technical fouls, yellow cards, and so on motivate the offending student-athlete? His or her teammates? Why or why not?

_____

_____

12. a. Research suggests negative group feedback, for example a coach yelling at the whole team when he or she is only mad at Jane, is a poor motivational technique. Do you agree or disagree?

_____

_____

b. How difficult is this for a coach to avoid doing?

_____

_____

13. How may motivating athletes differ in team and individual sports? Provide specific examples.

_____

_____

_____

14. Describe motivation by example.

_____

_____

_____

15. How does the respect a team has for a coach impact that coach's ability to motivate?

_____

_____

_____

16. a. How successful are fiery pre-game speeches as motivational tools? Fiery in-game speeches, such as during a time-out?

_____

_____

_____

b. Martens (2004) suggests the pre-game speech can do as much harm as good because some players will become too anxious and thus not be able to perform satisfactorily. Do you agree or disagree?

_____

_____

_____

17. Can a coach motivate student-athletes by competing against them in practice? Why or why not? What are the considerations?

_____

_____

_____

18. a. A coach has the responsibility to self-motivate. Describe some examples of how a coach may do this.

_____

_____

b. How successful can a coach be at hiding their lack of motivation?

_____

_____

c. What are coaches' responsibilities to themselves and their team if they perceive they are struggling to stay motivated, especially to attend practice?

_____

_____

d. What is a head coach's role in motivating assistant coaches?

_____

_____

Scenarios

1. Your volleyball team started the season well but has lost 11 of their last 13 matches and has fallen into the second division in the conference standings. Last night your team played poorly and without much effort as they lost to the league's last place team 25–17, 25–14. Today's practice is off to a bad start as there appears to be no effort—the team is simply playing out the schedule. You call for a water break while your coaching staff quickly huddles. Something has to change now. What do you do?

_____

_____

_____

_____

2. Your basketball team had struggled early in the season but has enjoyed a good stretch; last night they upset one of the top ranked teams in the state. You want the players to feel good about themselves, but also want them to realize there are several games left. How do you approach the next day's practice?

_____

_____

_____

_____

3. You are in your first season as a head coach. Your predecessor was someone who consistently used yelling, swearing, physical punishment, and threats as motivational tools. These tactics do not fit your personality or your philosophy. However, your athletes have taken your softer demeanor as an indicator you are not passionate about the team. How do you ensure your student-athletes this is not the case?

_____

_____

_____

_____

Practice Exercises

1. Reflect on the following statement Martens (2004) offers as the goal to enhance athletes' motivation: "A coach must find a way for every athlete to experience success in an environment in which winners are few and losers are many." Provide a half-page response as to how you can best do this for your team. Share your reflection with a colleague and critique each other's effort.

_____

_____

_____

_____

_____

_____

2. Create a list of what motivates you to continue coaching. Share your list with a colleague and review each other's effort.

_____

_____

_____

_____

_____

_____

_____

References

Brown, K.M. (1999). *Health locus of control.* University of South Florida Community and Family Health. Retrieved November 6, 2006 from http://hsc.usf.edu/~kmbrown/Locus_of_Control_Overview.htm.

Frank, M.A. (2002). *Feedback, self-efficacy, and the development of motor skills.* Retrieved November 9, 2006 from http://www.behavioralconsultants.com/feedback.htm.

Jensen, C.R., & Overman, S.J. (2003). *Administration and management of physical education and athletics* (4th ed.). Prospect Heights, IL: Waveland Press, Inc.

Kohl, T. (n.d.). *Six keys for motivating athletes.* Retrieved November 9, 2006 from http://www.tkohl.com/sixkeys.htm.

Lenti, F. (1996). *Motivating young athletes.* Gatorade Sports Science Institute. Retrieved August 2, 2006 from http://www.gssiweb.com/reflib/refs/93/d000000020000002f.cfm?pf=1&CFID=4453977&.

Martens, R. (2004). *Successful coaching* (3rd ed.). Champaign, IL: Human Kinetics.

Wuest, D.A., & Bucher, C.A. (2006). *Foundations of physical education, exercise and sport* (15th ed.). Boston: McGraw-Hill.

Self-confident athletes typically perform at higher levels, and their confidence may rub off on team-mates. Confident coaches are more likely to earn respect from their student-athletes and their peers, potentially leading to greater results.

Confidence can be defined as the belief in one's ability to be successful. This chapter investigates the coach's role in boosting his or her student-athlete's confidence. The next section defines self-efficacy, elaborates on where student-athletes derive it, and provides suggestions for coaches when attempting to inflate a player's confidence. The discussion questions ascertain when a coach may need to deflate a player's confidence, how the coach should consider the impact on a player's confidence when deciding whether to substitute for them, and what a coach should do when he or she does not have confidence in a particular player. The scenarios depict situations where a coach removes a player from a contest and where a coach has student-athletes that are both overconfident and lacking self-confidence.

This chapter also investigates a coach's confidence level and its importance to the program. Background information is provided on coaching efficacy and in what professional responsibilities coaches have the most and least confidence. The discussion questions include whether a coach who exudes self-confidence can truly be lacking in it and how student-athletes demonstrate whether or not they have confidence in a coach. Five of the seven scenarios present a coach with a situation when he or she is faced with important decisions during a game's culminating point.

Warm-Up

In this section coaches are introduced to the definition of self-efficacy and how athletes derive it. Strategies and psychological interventions to boost confidence in performance are provided. A section also describes areas where coaches themselves have both much and little self-efficacy.

1. Definitions of self-efficacy:
   a. The level of self-confidence in an individual's belief that he or she can successfully perform a specific activity given a particular situation (Frank, 2002).
   b. A person's confidence about his or her competence or abilities in a specific situation (Wuest & Bucher, 2006).

2. How an athlete's self-efficacy is derived (Frank, 2001):
   a. Previous experience
   b. Observation of others
   c. Verbal persuasion
   d. Physiological state of arousal

3. Psychological interventions used with athletes that may boost confidence in performance (Siedentop, 2004):

   a. Relaxation training

   b. Cue-controlled relaxation; having student-athletes relax upon a cue (auditory or visual)

   c. Mental imaging; rehearse mentally successful performance

   d. Coping strategies; predict what obstacles may occur to success and rehearse strategy to overcome

4. Coaching efficacy and where coaches rated high and low (Fung, 2003):

   a. Coaching efficacy is defined as "the extent to which coaches believe that they have the ability to enact behaviors and fulfill tasks expected of coaches."

   b. High school coaches were less confident in analyzing strengths and weaknesses of opposing teams, making decisions on game strategy, and maximizing athlete's strengths.

   c. High school coaches were more confident in their ability to instruct, motivate their student-athletes, and develop their athlete's character.

---

http://health.jbpub.com/book/prepare

Go to the web component of *Preparing the Successful Coach* at http://health.jbpub.com/book/prepare for web exercises and a suggested reading list.

Discussion Questions

1. a. Is it a coach's responsibility to build his or her student-athletes' confidence? Describe the balance between the coach's and the athlete's responsibility.

_____

_____

b. What, if any, is the role of teammates? How can they help or hinder a teammate's confidence?

_____

_____

_____

c. What, if any, is the role of a student-athlete's parents or others close to him or her? How can they help or hinder a teammate's confidence?

_____

_____

_____

2. a. How does a coach knowingly and unknowingly boost and/or hinder the student-athlete's confidence during games?

_____

_____

b. During practice?

_____

_____

_____

c. During the off-season?

_____

_____

_____

3. Describe the point where a coach repeatedly attempting to boost a player's confidence actually has a negative impact because the student-athlete no longer believes it to be genuine?

_____

_____

_____

_____

4. Are there times when a coach needs to deflate a player's confidence? If so, what is the correct approach?

_____

_____

_____

_____

5. a. How much should a coach consider the potential impact on a player's confidence when deciding to substitute for that player?

_____

_____

_____

b. What may be other considerations?

_____

_____

_____

c. Should a coach purposefully replace a player who had been struggling with his or her confidence immediately after successfully logging a solid series of plays or minutes so he or she ends the outing on a positive note? Why or why not?

_____

_____

_____

6. a. What should a coach do with the student-athlete who always needs verbal praises to boost his or her confidence?

_____

_____

_____

b. Are there student-athletes who want repeated praise as opposed to those who need it? What is the difference? How should a coach handle the former?

_____

_____

_____

7. What is meant when an athlete is described as having a quiet confidence?

_____

_____

_____

8. a. Describe the fine line between confidence and arrogance.

_____

_____

b. What is the coach's role in ensuring the line is not crossed?

_____

_____

_____

c. How easy is it for a coach to determine which student-athletes who exude arrogance truly believe in themselves as opposed to the student-athletes who exude arrogance to mask a lack of self-confidence? What are the differences between these two student-athletes and how a coach should approach them?

_____

_____

_____

9. a. What is a coach's responsibility when he or she does not have confidence in a student-athlete's ability to perform at the necessary level during a competition?

_____

_____

_____

b. How many mistakes should a coach allow a student-athlete to make before removing him or her from the game? How might the game's magnitude matter?

_____

_____

10. How can coaches attempt to inflate or deflate a team's confidence level when comparing them with an upcoming opponent? What are the advantages and disadvantages of attempting to do this?

_____

_____

_____

11. Critique Fung's results of her study on coaching efficacy. Would your personal experiences and interaction with fellow coaches lead you to accept or reject the professional responsibilities she cites as coaches having the most and least confidence? Why?

_____

_____

_____

_____

12. a. How important is self-confidence in a coach's ability to lead a successful program?

_____

_____

_____

b. Identify examples of what may bolster or weaken a coach's self-confidence.

_____

_____

_____

13. a. How does a coach display self-confidence?

_____

_____

_____

b. Can a self-confident coach still be unsure of him- or herself in certain key situations?

_____

_____

_____

c. Can a coach with little self-confidence successfully exude a confidence so that student-athletes and peers are fooled? Why or why not?

_____

_____

_____

14. How do student-athletes show confidence or no confidence in their coach?

_____

_____

_____

_____

Scenarios

1. Your football team is trailing by two points with 4 seconds remaining in the contest. Your team has the ball fourth and goal on your opponent's 5-yard line. Your kicker has already missed two field goals, and you presently have no confidence in his ability to make the winning kick. You elect to go for the touchdown as opposed to attempting a 22-yard field goal. How and when do you approach your kicker? Does it matter if you score the touchdown or not?

_____

_____

_____

2. Your soccer team was winning 4–0 with 20 minutes left when you entered your backup goalie in the game. Your opponent scored three goals in 15 minutes, and two of them were in part due to your goalie's poor decisions. Do you send your starter back in the game for the remaining 5 minutes? Should you consider whether the game is early in the season? A conference game? Your backup goalie's potential? How and when should you address your backup goalie if you replace her?

_____

_____

_____

a. What would deflate a player's confidence more: being removed from the game or remaining in the game and allowing the tying goal?

_____

_____

3. You were careful with your sophomore pitcher in the early portion of the season—picking spots for him to pitch where he would likely succeed so as to boost his confidence. He has pitched four quality innings in today's non-conference game but has run into trouble in the fifth inning with your team leading 5–1. There are two runners on base and the opponent's top of the order is coming to the plate. It appears your pitcher still has a lively arm. These are the types of situations he has to learn to pitch out of if he is going to take the next step in his growth as a pitcher. Simultaneously, you want him to end his outing with a sense of accomplishment. How do you proceed?

_____

_____

_____

4. Michelle is your volleyball team's defensive specialist. She did not play well in her last match, and your opponent continued to serve to her because Michelle was consistently unable to make a good pass. Michelle, normally a consistent performer, has been unable to shrug off this poor performance and has continued to struggle with receiving serves this week in practice. Her self-confidence is low heading into this evening's match; she is a player scared to have the other team serve to her. How do you proceed?

_____

_____

_____

5. Tommy is off to a 6–1 start as your number 4 singles player. You believe Tommy's record has gone to his head and he has become overconfident in his abilities. This weekend the team is playing in an invitational featuring the toughest competition to date. You believe Tommy is more concerned with the fact he has not been promoted to the number 3 singles slot than working on his game in preparation for the weekend. Your experience leads you to believe Tommy is in for a rude awakening. How might you approach him before the tournament? Will he have to learn the hard way?

_____

_____

_____

_____

6. Your team is playing the state's top-ranked team in the second round of the state playoffs. You want your team to have confidence in their ability to play with, and subsequently defeat, your opponent. You also realize your opponent is both extremely talented and well coached and is ranked number one for a reason. What approach do you take with your team? What if the situation was reversed and your squad was the state's top-ranked team?

_____

_____

_____

_____

7. Your team is involved in the final minutes, innings, or points of a close game. Key situations are about to occur where your decisions may be important to the game's outcome. How must you "carry yourself" when you make these decisions? How should you carry yourself both if your decisions lead to a victory or to a defeat?

_____

_____

_____

_____

Practice Exercise

1. Assess your confidence in your following coaching-related abilities: the play you have called in a tight situation is the right one; your ability to explain bad news, such as a reduction in playing time, to student-athletes in person; your ability to interact with peers in person; your ability to lead your program to the desired goals. Share your articulations with a colleague you trust and discuss each other's assessment.

_____

_____

_____

_____

_____

_____

EXERCISE 19.0

References

Frank, M.A. (2001). *Self-efficacy: The key to success in sports.* Retrieved November 9, 2006 from http://www.behavioralconsultants.com/self-efficacy.htm.

Frank, M.A. (2002). *Feedback, self-efficacy, and the development of motor skills.* Retrieved November 9, 2006 from http://www.behavioralconsultants.com/feedback.htm.

Fung, L. (2003, March). Assessment: Coaching efficacy as indicators of coach education program needs. *Athletic Insight: The Online Journal of Sport Psychology, 5*(1). Retrieved from http://www.athleticinsight.com/Vol5Iss1/CoachingEfficacy.htm.

Siedentop, D. (2004). *Introduction to physical education, fitness and sport* (5th ed.). Boston: McGraw-Hill.

Wuest, D.A., & Bucher, C.A. (2006). *Foundations of physical education, exercise science and sport* (15th ed.). Boston: McGraw-Hill.

Confrontation

A coach will be faced with confrontation, defined as a face-to-face meeting, during his or her career. How these confrontations or conflicts are handled may determine the success and longevity of a coach's career. Confrontation could occur with players, parents, colleagues, assistant coaches, opposing coaches, officials, administrators, or fans.

This chapter defines conflict, provides theory on conflict management, and provides strategies to minimize conflict. The discussion questions ask when a coach should apologize and when he or she should walk away from a situation. Twelve different scenarios are presented where coaches are asked how they would handle conflicts with different individuals.

Warm-Up

This section introduces coaches to the definition and ingredients of conflict. Strategies are offered on how to both minimize and manage the conflict coaches will undoubtedly encounter. Conflict can be healthy, and a section offers the results of such healthy conflict. The last section includes strategies coaches can use when faced with a confrontation.

1. Strategies to minimize and manage conflict (Stier, 1999):
   a. Recognize all conflict cannot be eliminated.
   b. Be proactive in recognizing sources of possible conflict.
   c. Remember to remain professional at all cost.
   d. Refrain from being judgmental in actions and communications.
   e. Attempt to understand the rationale for the dissent.

2. Definition of conflict: A natural disagreement resulting from individuals or groups that differ in attitudes, beliefs, values or needs. It can also originate from past rivalries and personality differences.

3. Ingredients of conflict:
   a. Needs—things essential to our well-being
   b. Perceptions—people interpret reality differently
   c. Power—an important influence on the types of conflict that occur
   d. Values—beliefs or principles we consider important
   e. Feelings and emotions—can differ over a particular issue; sometimes people ignore their own or others' feelings or emotions

4. Results of healthy conflict:
   a. Growth and innovation
   b. New ways of thinking
   c. Additional options

5. Managing conflict (Hoban, n.d.):

   a. Analyze the conflict

   b. Determine the management strategy

      i. Collaboration

      ii. Compromise

      iii. Competition

      iv. Accommodation

      v. Avoidance

   c. Pre-negotiation

   d. Negotiation

   e. Post-negotiation

6. Strategies when faced with a confrontation:

   a. Keep your assistants or other persons in the proximity if you believe there is potential for a confrontation to get out of hand.

   b. Use whatever strategy that fits your personality to avoid or minimize the confrontation.

   c. Do not follow someone who is attempting to walk away from the confrontation.

   d. Document situations that necessitate it.

---

http://health.jbpub.com/book/prepare

Go to the web component of *Preparing the Successful Coach* at http://health.jbpub.com/book/prepare for web exercises and a suggested reading list.

Discussion Questions

1. a. What should administrators, parents, and student-athletes expect from a coach when they are involved in a confrontation, both during and afterward?

_____

_____

_____

b. Provide examples of a coach's behavior that may warrant disciplinary action? A warning?

_____

_____

_____

c. How may the number of confrontations a coach has been involved with impact the decision to exonerate, warn, or discipline him or her?

_____

_____

_____

2. a. Does society expect coaches to be somewhat confrontational? Are coaches who attempt to avoid confrontation, especially with game officials, characterized as not being passionate or as being unwilling to stick up for their student-athletes?

_____

_____

_____

b. How may such societal expectations place pressure on coaches?

_____

_____

c. What behavior would society expect of a coach when involved in a confrontation with any of the following constituents?
   i. His or her student-athletes?

_____

_____

   ii. Opposing student-athletes or coaches?

_____

_____

   iii. Fans?

_____

_____

   iv. Game officials?

_____

_____

   v. Administrators?

_____

_____

   vi. Assistant coaches?

_____

_____

3. Under what circumstances should a coach apologize for his or her behavior stemming from a confrontation? Under what circumstances should a coach expect an apology?

_____

_____

_____

4. a. Swearing may occur during a confrontation. What is a coach's responsibility if he or she swears? Are sworn at during the conflict?

_____

_____

_____

b. Does it matter if others, especially players, are within earshot of the conversation?

_____

_____

5. a. Under what circumstances is a coach justified in walking away from a confrontation?

_____

_____

b. Is a coach ever justified in pursuing someone who is walking away from him or her?

_____

_____

_____

6. How difficult is it to not hold a grudge against someone with whom you had a nasty confrontation?

_____

_____

_____

_____

Scenarios

1. How should a coach respond in the following situations?
a. Situation with student-athlete: You have sent in a substitute for the student-athlete. The student-athlete shouts, "Why are you taking me out?" as he or she walks off the competition area. The student-athlete then shouts to no one in particular in the crowd, "Do any of you want to coach this team? You can't do any worse!"

_____

_____

b. Situation with coworker: It is your team's turn to have the practice area. You walk up to the head coach of the team currently using it and politely say, "Coach, it's 4:32—we are supposed to be on the court." The coach turns to you and rudely says, "Relax, we will be off in 5 minutes."

_____

_____

c. Situation with an opposing coach: Your team has just upset a state-ranked opponent on your home field. The opposing coach believes the officiating was poor. The coach approaches you for the post-game handshake and says, "We aren't coming back if you can't find competent officials. No way you beat us in a fair game."

_____

_____

d. Situation with an opposing player: An opposing player believes she just suffered a cheap shot at the hands of one of your student-athletes, but you honestly believe it was inadvertent. She shouts in your direction while the game is being played, "Coach, you better take her out of the game or I will."

_____

_____

e. Situation with a parent after a game: Their daughter, a senior who played more last year under a different coach, has not played in the team's first six games. "Coach, I want to know what horrible things our daughter has done to you that you have such little respect for her and don't play her in games. Are you that incompetent that you believe she isn't one of your better players?"

_____

_____

f. Situation with a fan, who is sitting close to your family: "Coach, you suck! Get your head out of your ass and call a freaking play that might actually work." The fan turns to your family and asks, "Is he this stupid at home?"

_____

_____

g. Situation with an official: An official has just made an incorrect interpretation of the rules and you politely inform him or her of your desire to challenge the decision. The official responds, "Coach, I know the rules and you don't. Now sit down and shut your mouth or I will run you."

_____

_____

h. Situation with principal: You accidentally left some valuable equipment outside yesterday. Fortunately, it was not stolen or damaged and you know you made a mistake. The principal sees you in the hall between classes and says, "Coach, you are lucky the equipment wasn't stolen. I need to be confident I have employees who can be responsible and don't leave things all over the place."

_____

_____

i. Situation with a stranger: Your team is eating a post-game meal at a fast food restaurant. They have been unruly but you have cut them some slack after enjoying a big victory. A restaurant patron approaches you and says, "I don't appreciate your kids being loud and throwing ice. What is the name of your supervisor?"

_____

_____

j. Situation with the bus driver: Your team is behind schedule in getting to the site for this evening's game. You frustratingly ask the bus driver if he can go a little faster. He responds quickly and curtly, "I don't tell you what plays to call, don't tell me how to drive."

_____

_____

k. Situation with a faculty colleague: A colleague is unhappy with your decision to allow one of your student-athletes to play despite being caught skipping afternoon classes. "Coach, you are sending a message to the teachers at this school that what we do doesn't matter. Don't underestimate the support you will need from us to receive tenure."

_____

_____

l. Situation with an assistant coach: Your assistant coach had told you something about a student-athlete in confidence and is now unhappy you plan to approach the student-athlete concerning the matter. "This is bulls**t. How do you expect the players to trust me when you cut my legs out from under me? I will have to think twice about telling you when a player comes to me with something confidential!"

_____

_____

_____

Practice Exercise

1. Assess your temper and how quick you would be to enter, avoid, and stray from conflict. Do you have concerns with your ability to appropriately handle conflict after this self-assessment? Share your articulations with a colleague you trust and discuss each other's assessment.

_____

_____

_____

_____

_____

_____

_____

References

Hoban, T.J. (n.d.). *Managing conflict: A guide for watershed partnerships.* Retrieved November 9, 2006 from http://www2.ctic.purdue.edu/KYW/Brochures/ManageConflict.html.

Stier, W.F. (1999). *Managing sport, fitness and recreation programs: Concepts and practices.* Boston: Allyn and Bacon.

Team
Physiology

21

Playing Injured Players

Several high schools and other amateur sport entities do not provide any athletic training or related medical service. Coaches are left to care for and make decisions concerning a player's injuries. These decisions are often outside of their expertise.

This chapter provides insight into the coach's role in the decision whether or not an injured student-athlete should play and the coach's status on the hierarchical chart compared with the athletic trainer or other members of the medical staff. Also included are guidelines for team sports medicine services and a Bill of Rights for injured student-athletes.

The chapter also looks at several other issues concerning injured student-athletes. The discussion questions ask coaches whether injured players should travel with the team and how much medical training coaches have a responsibility to obtain. The scenarios provide examples surrounding the decision whether an injured student-athlete should play.

This chapter also reviews the coach's responsibility to ensure student-athletes practice in safe conditions, especially during extreme heat. Three discussion scenarios address this issue, and a practice exercise allows coaches to prepare a practice schedule during such conditions.

Warm-Up

This section introduces coaches to multiple issues surrounding injured student-athletes. The first part provides general guidelines for team sports medicine services. The next part describes components of the ideal relationship between several constituents involved in the decision of when an injured student-athlete can return to action. Flint's Bill of Rights of injured student-athletes is provided, and the section concludes with recommendations to prevent dehydration in student-athletes.

1. Guidelines for team sports medicine services (Appenzeller, 1993):
    a. Coaches should not be allowed to overrule an athletic trainer or team doctor's decision concerning whether or not a student-athlete can participate.
        i. The head coach and the sports medicine coordinator must be equal on the hierarchical chart, with both reporting directly to the athletic director; trainers are not to report directly to coaches.
    b. A coach who does overrule an athletic trainer must be informed they can and will be held legally responsible for further injury to the student-athlete.
    c. A policy manual should be available for all coaches and sports medicine staff.
    d. A medical history for each student-athlete should be compiled and maintained.
        i. A thorough physical exam should be required of all student-athletes before participation.

© 2008 Jones and Bartlett Publishers, Inc.   www.jbpub.com

    e. An emergency plan, including readily available phone numbers of emergency personnel, should be prepared and available.

    f. The sports medicine staff must address pre-existing conditions.

2. The ideal relationship between the coach, athletic trainer, team physician, and student-athlete (Prentice & Arnheim, 2005):

    a. The primary concern of everyone must be the athlete.

    b. The physician assumes the responsibility of making the decisions from the time of the injury until full return.

    c. The coach must defer and support the decisions of medical experts.

    d. Coaches should assist the athletic trainer to create appropriate drills during a student-athlete's rehabilitation.

    e. The coach and the athletic trainer must have mutual respect for each other's job.

3. Flint's Bill of Rights for injured athletes (Voyageur Athletics [Laurentian University Athletic Department], n.d.):

    a. Receive appropriate and immediate medical attention.

    b. Receive moral and informed information concerning the athlete's return to play after an injury.

    c. Receive protection from injury and re-injury.

4. Recommendations to prevent dehydration during exercise (Powers & Howley, 2004):

    a. Athletes should be hydrated before practice.

    b. Athletes should consume 150–300 ml of fluid every 15 to 20 minutes during exercise.

    c. Athletes should monitor fluid losses by recording body weight before and after a workout. Athletes should consume fluids equal to 150% of the weight lost.

    d. Athletes should monitor the color of their urine. Urine is dark yellow in dehydrated individuals.

http://health.jbpub.com/book/prepare

Go to the web component of *Preparing the Successful Coach* at http://health.jbpub.com/book/prepare for web exercises and a suggested reading list.

Discussion Questions

1. a. Who should be included in the decision concerning whether an injured student-athlete should play? What say should each individual have? Who should make the final decision?

_____

_____

_____

    b. Should a policy specifically delineating how such situations are handled exist?

_____

_____

_____

2. How should a coach proceed if a player's personal physician has a different opinion from the school's doctor or athletic trainer?

_____

_____

_____

3. Do coaches pressure trainers and doctors to get a student-athlete ready to play? What crosses the line? Provide specific examples.

_____

_____

_____

_____

4. Some schools may contract their athletic training services to an outside agency, resulting in several different trainers covering events throughout the course of the season. How may such an arrangement impact the relationship a coach can develop with the trainers?

_____

_____

_____

_____

5. a. Prentice and Arnheim (2005) stipulate all coaches should be trained in cardiopulmonary resuscitation (CPR) and first aid. Do you agree or disagree?

_____

_____

_____

b. What medical training should coaches be expected to have? Why?

_____

_____

_____

c. Who should be expected to pay for such training—the school or the coach?

_____

_____

_____

6. States have different laws governing what non-medical personnel can and cannot do when providing health care. Who should have the primary responsibility to be educated on their state's laws—the coach or the administration? Why?

_____

_____

_____

_____

7. a. A common guideline is that a student-athlete who is too hurt to play should sit out. If they are not too hurt to play, then a student-athlete should not use his or her injury or illness as an excuse for poor performance. Is this fair?

_____

_____

_____

b. What strategies can a coach use to ensure student-athletes do not use injuries as an excuse?

_____

_____

_____

_____

© 2008 Jones and Bartlett Publishers, Inc.   www.jbpub.com

8. a. Are players who are hurt or sick but do not tell anyone tough, stupid, or both?

_____

_____

b. What type of players does a coach want?

_____

_____

9. What do coaches mean when they say there is a difference between being injured and being hurt? Do coaches have different expectations of these student-athletes?

_____

_____

_____

10. How should a coach handle a student-athlete coming off a serious injury who is timid at first?

_____

_____

_____

11. Can student-athletes miss parts of practice to complete therapy or rehabilitation, or should that be on their own time?

_____

_____

_____

12. a. Should a coach expect injured players to attend games?

_____

_____

b. Does it matter if the game is home or away?

_____

_____

c. Does it matter if the game is scheduled for a school night or weekend?

_____

_____

d. Does it matter if it is a team sport or an individual sport?

_____

_____

_____

e. Does it matter if the injury is season-ending or not?

_____

_____

_____

13. Who should be included in the decision whether a student-athlete with a pre-existing medical condition (such as a heart condition) is allowed to participate? Who should have the final say?

_____

_____

_____

_____

14. What responsibility does a coach have, in the absence of an athletic trainer, to ensure student-athletes practice in safe weather conditions?

_____

_____

_____

_____

15. What precautions should coaches take during practices in extreme heat?

_____

_____

_____

_____

16. What type of communication should occur between a coach and athletic trainer concerning practices during extreme heat? Who should have the final say in whether to reschedule, shorten, or cancel a practice? Why?

_____

_____

_____

17. What are each of the following individual's responsibilities to ensure a positive working relationship between the coach and the athletic trainer?
a. The coach?

_____

_____

b. The athletic trainer?

_____

_____

c. The athletic director?

_____

_____

_____

Scenarios

1. Your school has a contract with a local athletic training provider. A college intern is covering your game today and has advised you that your injured student-athlete should not re-enter the game. The student-athlete, a key player, tells you he is ready to play. What do you do?

_____

_____

_____

_____

2. a. Your school is in a conference that requires 90-minute trips (one way) to several conference opponents. Lisa is one of your volleyball team's starting outside hitters and she recently sustained an injury that will sideline her the next 5 weeks. Lisa and her mother approach you, asking that Lisa be dismissed from attending the three conference road matches that occur on Tuesday evenings so she can attend to her studies. The team would not be scheduled to return on those evenings until 11:00 P.M. How do you respond?

_____

_____

_____

b. How would you respond if Lisa was a third-string player on the volleyball team? Your number 4 singles player in tennis?

_____

_____

_____

3. Dani is the starting mid-fielder on your soccer team that is now in the middle of the season. She is a talented player but has a reputation among her teammates of not practicing hard and overall not being mentally tough. Dani played the entire game yesterday and today comes to you and says she has shin splints. She would like the next 2 days off of practice so her shins are rested for your game in 3 days. There is no athletic trainer at your school, so the decision is yours. How do you proceed? What are the considerations?

_____

_____

_____

Practice Exercise

1. You are the coach for a fall outdoor sport. You are in the pre-season and are hoping to practice twice a day for the next week. Your varsity, junior varsity, and freshmen squad all share one practice site. The forecast is calling for record-breaking heat. Prepare a 6-day schedule (assume no practice on Sunday) for all three squads while considering this forecast. Share your schedule with a colleague and critique each other's efforts.

_____

_____

_____

_____

_____

_____

_____

_____

_____

References

Appenzeller, H. (1993). *Managing sports and risk management strategies.* Durham, NC: Carolina Academic Press.

Powers, S.K., & Howley, E.T. (2004). *Exercise physiology: Theory and application to fitness and performance* (5th ed.). Boston: McGraw-Hill.

Prentice, W.E., & Arnheim, D.D. (2005). *Essentials of athletic injury management* (6th ed.). Boston: McGraw-Hill.

Voyageur Athletics student-athlete return-to-play policy. (n.d.). Retrieved August 10, 2006 from http://laurentian.ca/vpacademic/POLICIES/VOYAGEURS.pdf

CHAPTER

22

Body Composition

Student-athletes are often willing to attempt multiple methods to gain a competitive edge, including altering their body composition through their diet and/or excessive conditioning.

This chapter provides research on eating disorders and the Female Athlete Triad. Recommendations for coaches concerning student-athletes and weight fluctuation are also included. The chapter investigates coach's actions that potentially lead a student-athlete toward an eating disorder. The discussion questions ask what responsibility a coach has to prevent and identify eating disorders and whether tactics such as weighing student-athletes, conducting body fat tests, and manipulating diet are appropriate. The scenarios include situations where student-athletes either want to or perceive they need to lose weight.

Conflicting research exists on the physical effects of exercise on a pregnant mother and the fetus. This chapter cites research outlining safe physical activity during pregnancy. A discussion question and scenario on pregnant student-athletes are provided.

Warm-Up

In this section coaches are introduced to various information pertaining to body composition. Recommendations concerning a student-athlete's possible decision to lose weight are offered. The Female Athlete Triad and examples of eating disorders are cited. The section concludes with information concerning safe physical activity for pregnant student-athletes.

1. Recommendations for decisions regarding student-athlete weight loss (Sabock, 2005):
   a. The coach and student-athlete should both be involved and the appropriate medical and nutritional personnel should be consulted.
   b. Weight-loss plans should be developed on an individual basis.

2. The Female Athlete Triad (Donatelle, 2004):
   a. A combination of disordered eating, cessation of menstruation (amenorrhea), and osteoporosis
   b. An often unrecognized disorder in females, particularly those who are physically active and especially for those in competitive sports where self-discipline is valued (gymnastics, cross-country, swimming, etc.)
   c. Behavioral warning signs
      i. Depression
      ii. Use of weight-loss products
      iii. Decreased ability to concentrate
      iv. Excessive and compulsive exercise
      v. Preoccupation with food and weight

      vi. Trips to bathroom during or after eating

      vii. Increased self-criticism

   d. Physical warning signs

      i. Fatigue

      ii. Anemia

      iii. Tendency toward stress fracture and injury

      iv. Cold intolerance

      v. Changes in endurance, strength, or speed

3. Categories of eating disorders (Donatelle, 2004):

   a. Anorexia nervosa, which is characterized by excessive preoccupation with food, self-starvation, and extreme exercising to achieve weight loss

      i. Additional characteristics include individuals who refuse to maintain the minimum body weight for one's height and age, have an intense fear of gaining weight, have a disturbed perception of one's body weight, and who miss three consecutive menstrual cycles.

   b. Bulimia nervosa, which is characterized by binge eating followed by inappropriate measures, such as purging, to prevent weight gain

4. Safe physical activity during pregnancy (Edlin & Golanty, 2007):

   a. Safe for beginners: walking, swimming, cycling, low-impact aerobics, prenatal yoga

   b. Safe for experienced exercisers: running, racquet sports, strength training

   c. Unsafe: contact sports, scuba diving

---

http://health.jbpub.com/book/prepare

Go to the web component of *Preparing the Successful Coach* at http://health.jbpub.com/book/prepare for web exercises and a suggested reading list.

Discussion Questions

1. a. Should coaches administer body fat tests? Why or why not?

_____

_____

_____

   b. Should the athletic trainer or team physician? If so, how should this individual relay the results to the coach? Should they at all?

_____

_____

_____

   c. Some argue such tests are necessary in some sports. Do you agree?

_____

_____

_____

2. a. Should coaches have student-athletes weigh in on a regular basis? Why or why not?

_____

_____

_____

b. Should the athletic trainer or team physician? If so, how should this individual relay the results to the coach? Should they at all?

_____

_____

_____

c. Some argue weighing in is necessary in some sports? Do you agree?

_____

_____

_____

d. Should punitive measures (not allowed to practice, extra conditioning) be implemented for student-athletes who do not make the desired weight? What are the dangers with such measures?

_____

_____

_____

3. Should a coach talk to a student-athlete about his or her weight or body composition? If so, under what conditions? What precautions should a coach take during such a conversation?

_____

_____

_____

_____

4. a. Does playing weight impact performance? How?

_____

_____

_____

b. Does losing weight guarantee an athlete will become more physically fit?

_____

_____

_____

c. Does gaining weight guarantee an athlete will become stronger?

_____

_____

_____

5. a. What is a coach's responsibility if he or she suspects a student-athlete has an eating disorder?

_____

_____

_____

b. Does a coach have a responsibility to be trained in recognizing eating disorders?

_____

_____

_____

6. a. What is a coach's responsibility on educating his or her student-athletes about proper nutrition and diet? Educating him- or herself?

_____

_____

b. Is it within a coach's authority to mandate a particular diet? Why or why not?

_____

_____

c. Should a coach have more control in selecting the meals student-athletes will consume if the team's budget is paying? Why or why not?

_____

_____

_____

7. What is a coach's responsibility if he or she suspects a female student-athlete is pregnant? What if he or she discovers the suspicion is fact?

_____

_____

_____

_____

Scenarios

1. You are the girl's volleyball coach at your school. You also serve as a lunchroom monitor. You notice most of your players do not eat healthy foods during lunch; they eat junk food and candy. Your players are in good physical condition and none of them has a weight problem. What should you do?

_____

_____

_____

2. a. One of your wrestlers comes to you 2 months before the beginning of the pre-season. He wants to go down two weight classes where he perceives he has a better chance to compete in varsity matches. His perception is likely correct. How do you counsel this student-athlete?

_____

_____

b. How would you counsel the football player who wants to move from linebacker to defensive end next season?

_____

_____

_____

3. You are the girl's soccer coach at your school. You have an athlete who in your professional opinion could increase her speed and endurance if she lost 10 to 15 pounds. How do you counsel this student-athlete?

_____

_____

_____

4. Julie was your starting second baseman as a junior; she had an athletic and healthy physique. Tryouts for this year have begun and you have noticed Julie does not possess the same energy she did last year. Her range up the middle and her ability to drive the ball has been diminished. Your program does not weigh the players, but you would estimate she has lost 20 pounds. You articulate this to your assistant, who replies that some of Julie's teammates suspect Julie has an eating disorder. How do you proceed?

_____

_____

_____

5. Kathryn is a senior on your swimming team who competes in two events. Kathryn and her parents arrange to meet with you and at this meeting inform you Kathryn is in the first trimester of a pregnancy. Kathryn realizes her times will not be fast enough to advance her past the first round of the post-season competitions and thus her season has 3 weeks and four meets left. She and her parents inform you her doctor has cleared her to continue competing these last 3 weeks and that her performance should not be adversely affected. Thus she expects to participate in meets as before. How do you proceed?

_____

_____

_____

Practice Exercise

1. Prepare dietary guidelines for your team during the season. Include foods and caloric intake that is both advised and not advised. Continue with your personal philosophy as to how much, or how, your recommended diet should be enforced and why. Share your thoughts with a colleague and discuss each other's assessment.

_____

_____

_____

_____

_____

_____

_____

References

Donatelle, R.J. (2004). *Access to health* (8th ed.). San Francisco: Pearson Education Inc.

Edlin, G., & Golanty, E. (2007). *Health & wellness* (9th ed.). Sudbury, MA: Jones and Bartlett Publishers.

Sabock, R.J. (2005). *Coaching: A realistic perspective* (8th ed.). San Diego: Collegiate Press.

CHAPTER

23

Ergogenic Aids

Ergogenic aids include anything that improves or is thought to improve performance. These are commonly thought of as legal and illegal supplements, but the definition is much broader. Ergogenic aids can include equipment, clothing, or altered mechanics.

This chapter provides information on different categories of ergogenic aids and summarizes the physiological and moral aspects of supplementation. A definition of ergogenic aids and information concerning anabolic steroids are also included.

Supplementation is emphasized in this chapter and discussion questions on the coach's responsibility to become educated in this area are provided. The discussion questions also delineate a coach's responsibility to educate his or her student-athletes and enforce team policies. The scenario depicts a situation where a coach must confront the realization members of the team are using an illegal substance. A practice exercise affords a coach an opportunity to create a policy concerning supplementation.

Warm-Up

A definition of ergogenic aids is provided as are descriptions and examples of the five categories. Additional sections provide a summary of ergogenic aid's effects and research on the morality of their use. Anabolic steroids are also discussed and information on their use is available.

1. Definition of ergogenic aid: Any substance, process, or procedure that may, or is perceived to, enhance athletic performance through improved strength, speed, response time or endurance.

2. Categories of ergogenic aids (Foss & Keteyian, 1998):
   a. Pharmacological—over-the-counter and illegal supplements
   b. Nutritional—diet, vitamin supplementation
   c. Physiological—conditioning, blood doping
   d. Psychological—hypnosis, suggestion, rehearsal
   e. Mechanical—clothing, equipment, body mechanics

3. Summary of effects of ergogenic aids (Powers & Howley, 2004):
   a. Little evidence exists that nutritional or pharmacological supplements provide a performance advantage, with the possible exception of creatine.
   b. Oxygen breathing before or after exercise has little or no effect on performance.
   c. Amphetamines do not improve the performance of alert, motivated, and nonfatigued athletes.
   d. Caffeine's ergogenic effect on performance varies to dose and is less pronounced in subjects who use caffeine daily.

4. Information on anabolic steroids (Edlin & Golanty, 2007):

  a. Anabolic steroids are synthetic derivatives of the male hormone testosterone.

  b. Anabolic steroids may be consumed orally or injected. They are usually taken in cycles.

  c. Anabolic steroids provide the ability to train longer and harder, subsequently allowing for increased lean muscle mass and strength.

  d. Side effects include liver tumors, jaundice, fluid retention, and high blood pressure.

  e. Side effects specific to men include shrinking testicles, reduced sperm count, infertility, baldness, and breast development.

  f. Side effects specific to women include changes of the menstrual cycle, clitoris enlargement, and deepened voice.

5. Ergogenic aids and morality (Lumpkin, Stoll, & Beller, 1999):

  a. The use of stimulants, depressants, anabolic steroids, and non-drug artificial substances is morally questionable because it provides users with unfair advantages.

  b. Athletes competing against other athletes are the essence of sport; thus creating an artificial imbalance by ingesting an ergogenic aid that reduces or masks fatigue or provides psychological advantages is unethical.

  c. The replacement of fluids and eating a balanced and nutritious diet to positively impact performance is not questionable ethically.

---

http://health.jbpub.com/book/prepare

Go to the web component of *Preparing the Successful Coach* at http://health.jbpub.com/book/prepare for web exercises and a suggested reading list.

Discussion Questions

1. Identify further examples for each of the categories of ergogenic aids.

_____

_____

_____

_____

2. Do you agree with Lumpkin, Stoll, and Beller's (1999) pronouncements on ergogenic aids? Explain your answer.

_____

_____

_____

_____

3. a. How should a coach counsel student-athletes concerning the use of legal supplements?

_____

_____

  b. Should a coach endorse their use, disallow their use, or remain neutral?

_____

_____

_____

c. Should coaches make their opinions known before being asked?

_____

_____

d. Who needs to be involved in the student-athlete's decision to use legal supplementation?

_____

_____

e. What, if any, communication should occur between a coach and the following constituents if one of his or her student-athletes plans on using legal supplementation: athletic director, athletic trainer, team physician?

_____

_____

_____

f. Does a coach have the authority to stipulate legal supplements cannot be taken? Should he or she exercise that authority?

_____

_____

_____

g. Does a coach have the authority to stipulate legal supplements must be taken?

_____

_____

_____

4. a. Does a coach have a responsibility to educate his or her student-athletes on the current research regarding supplement use?

_____

_____

_____

b. How much expertise should a coach be expected to have in this area?

_____

_____

c. How easy should it be for a coach to detect whether a student-athlete is using supplements?

_____

_____

5. What should a coach do upon discovering a player is using an illegal supplement? A legal supplement the coach would prefer not be consumed?

_____

_____

_____

6. Ergogenic aids, by definition, include equipment. How much should coaches encourage student-athletes to spend top dollar on the best equipment (baseball bats, golf clubs, tennis rackets, swim suits, etc.)?

_____

_____

_____

_____

Scenario

1. You are the football coach at your school. The custodian approaches you one morning with materials he inadvertently found in the trash. They include syringes and vials of anabolic steroids. This surprises you because you have not noticed any of your student-athletes making excessive gains in body mass or strength. How do you approach this situation?

_____

_____

_____

_____

Practice Exercise

1. Create a policy concerning your student-athletes and legal and illegal supplements. What products will you allow them to take? Not allow them to take? How must student-athletes inform you of what they are consuming? What are penalties for violating this policy? Share your thoughts with a colleague and critique each other's efforts.

_____

_____

_____

_____

_____

_____

_____

References

Edlin, G., & Golanty, E. (2007). *Health & wellness* (9th ed.). Sudbury, MA: Jones and Bartlett Publishers.

Foss, M., & Keteyian, S. (1998). *Fox's physiological basis for exercise and sport* (6th ed.). Boston: McGraw-Hill.

Lumpkin, A., Stoll, S.K., & Beller, J.M. (1999). *Sport ethics: Applications for fair play* (2nd ed.). Boston: McGraw-Hill.

Powers, S.K., & Howley, E.T. (2004). *Exercise physiology: Theory and application to fitness and performance* (5th ed.). Boston: McGraw-Hill.

CHAPTER
24

Alcohol, Tobacco, and Illicit Drugs

Research reveals the use of alcohol and drugs among high school students is decreasing but remains prevalent (National Center for Chronic Disease Prevention and Health Promotion, n.d.). Coaches implicitly and explicitly reveal their tolerance for this illegal behavior through their words and actions.

This chapter discusses a coach's role in educating his or her athletes about alcohol, drugs, and tobacco and how strict he or she should be concerning its use and abuse. Background information defines important terms, identifies recommendations to prevent student-athlete alcohol use, and details the effects of alcohol use on the body.

The discussion questions ask what a coach's alcohol policy should be in the absence of a school policy and how a coach should review his or her own personal drinking habits. The discussion questions also identify illegal drug and tobacco use as concerns.

The scenarios offer five different situations involving alcohol and one involving tobacco. These include critiquing both coaches' and student-athletes' use of alcohol and tobacco products. The chapter concludes with a practice exercise that asks coaches to define their policy toward alcohol, tobacco, and drug use.

Warm-Up

This section introduces coaches to important information on how they should handle the alcohol use of their student-athletes. Recommendations for administrators are provided on how to prevent alcohol use among student-athletes. Physiological research on the implications of alcohol use on the body within 48 hours of consumption is also provided.

1. Recommendations for administrators and coaches to prevent alcohol use by student-athletes (Dowdall, 2003):
   a. Require coaches to talk to their athletes about the dangers of alcohol and the social pressures to use it.
   b. Encourage coaches to attend workshops that instruct them on the best way to approach the subject with their student-athletes.
   c. A clear expectation that alcohol is prohibited, along with clearly defined consequences, must be delineated.

2. Implications of alcohol use on athletes within 48 hours of consumption (Robson, n.d.):
   a. Decreases strength
   b. Impairs reaction time

c. Impacts liver function, resulting in increased fatigue

d. Depletes aerobic capacity, resulting in decreased endurance

e. Interferes with quality sleep

3. Important related definitions (Edlin & Golanty, 2007):

a. Drug abuse: excessive use of a drug without medical reasons

b. Addiction: physical and psychological dependence on a substance or behavior

c. Tolerance: condition in which increased amounts of a drug are required to produce desired effects

---

http://health.jbpub.com/book/prepare

Go to the web component of *Preparing the Successful Coach* at http://health.jbpub.com/book/prepare for web exercises and a suggested reading list.

Discussion Questions

1. a. What should a coach's philosophy be toward high school athletes and the use of alcohol?

_____

_____

_____

b. Should coaches exude a proactive, no tolerance message or a "Don't be stupid" approach? What are the differences in how student-athletes will react?

_____

_____

_____

c. Do you agree with Dowdall (2003) that a coach has a responsibility to educate his or her athletes concerning the dangers of alcohol?

_____

_____

_____

2. a. What are appropriate alcohol rules and consequences for a coach to implement in the absence of a school policy?

_____

_____

_____

b. Should rules be applicable only in-season? Why or why not?

_____

_____

_____

c. Should a coach be able to implement consequences that exceed those set in a school policy?

_____

_____

_____

3. Does a coach have a responsibility to address a situation when he or she overhears student-athletes talking about past drinking escapades? Future drinking escapades?

_____

_____

_____

4. a. What is a coach's responsibility if he or she receives a call from a parent informing him or her of last weekend's drinking party? This upcoming weekend's?

_____

_____

_____

b. What evidence does a coach need to pursue an allegation?

_____

_____

_____

c. What evidence does a coach need to impose punishment?

_____

_____

_____

5. a. What should a coach do if he or she suspects a student-athlete may have a drinking problem? A drug problem?

_____

_____

_____

b. What characteristics will a student-athlete display that may make a coach suspicious the student-athlete may have a problem?

_____

_____

_____

c. Should a coach be expected to notice warning signs of an alcohol or drug problem? Why or why not?

_____

_____

_____

6. What should a coach's philosophy be toward high school athletes and the use of illegal drugs?

_____

_____

_____

7. a. What should a coach's philosophy be toward high school athletes and the use of tobacco products?

_____

_____

_____

b. Baseball players are generalized to be more likely to use and abuse smokeless tobacco. Should a baseball coach be more vigilant in his or her philosophy? Why or why not?

_____

_____

8. a. What responsibility does a coach have in his or her own personal drinking habits?

_____

_____

b. Is it appropriate for a coach to discuss drinking war stories with student-athletes?

_____

_____

c. Should a coach purchase or consume alcohol publicly in his or her community?

_____

_____

d. How may a coach's responsibility change when his or her kids are in high school?

_____

_____

e. How may a coach's alcohol use impact how his or her student-athletes perceive him or her?

_____

_____

9. Is it acceptable for a coach to use tobacco products? Why or why not?

_____

_____

_____

10. What should a coach do if he or she suspects a player has arrived at a game or practice hung-over or intoxicated?

_____

_____

_____

Scenarios

1. You are the high school track and field coach and your daughter runs on the team. She calls you at 1:00 A.M. to pick her up from a party because she and her friends, all members of the track team, are too intoxicated to drive. These student-athletes are all violating the team rule prohibiting drinking. The student-athletes believe they should not be punished because you would never have known about this incident if you were not also the parent of an athlete. How do you handle this situation?

_____

_____

_____

2. You are at the local grocery store during a slow time. You had planned on purchasing a 12-pack of beer but the only lane open is being checked by one of your student-athletes. Do you proceed to buy the alcohol? Why or why not?

_____

_____

_____

3. You arrive at the local fast-food restaurant after a late night of scouting. You see one of your players, and he appears to be intoxicated. How do you handle this situation?

_____

_____

_____

4. Your school has a policy where a student-athlete must miss one-third of a season for a second alcohol offense. You are a softball coach and one of your players incurred her second offense during the fall. This athlete has not played basketball in the past, but she plans to go out for basketball, serve her suspension in that sport, and then quit the team. How do you advise this student-athlete?

_____

_____

_____

5. You are hosting a family Memorial Day picnic. Your son is in high school and wants to invite friends, who happen to play for you, to the gathering. It is common for alcohol to be served at your family functions and for you to drink beer with your barbecue. Do you do anything different this year with your son's friends at the party?

_____

_____

_____

6. You are leaving a movie theatre on a Saturday night when you see one of your student-athletes smoking a cigarette. You do not have a team rule concerning the use of tobacco products because you erroneously thought you did not need one. How do you handle this situation?

_____

_____

_____

Practice Exercise

1. Place in writing your alcohol, drug, and tobacco policy toward three different constituents: your student-athletes, your assistant coaches, and yourself. Include consequences with your expectations. Share these with a colleague and critique each other's efforts.

_____

_____

_____

_____

_____

_____

_____

References

Dowdall, M.P. (2003). *Coaches' attitudes and behaviors towards alcohol prevention among male high school athletes.* Unpublished master's thesis, University of Cincinnati. Retrieved November 9, 2006 from http://www.ohiolink.edu/etd/view.cgi?acc_num=ucin1046804612.

Edlin, G., & Golanty, E. (2007). *Health & Wellness* (9th ed.). Sudbury, MA: Jones and Bartlett Publishers.

National Center for Chronic Disease Prevention and Health Promotion. (n.d.). *Healthy youth: Alcohol and drug use.* Retrieved November 9, 2006 from http://www.cdc. gov/HealthyYouth/alcoholdrug/index.htm.

Robson, D. (n.d.). *Bodybuilding and alcohol: Do they mix?* Retrieved November 9, 2006 from http://www.bodybuilding.com/fun/drobson11.htm.

EXERCISE 24.0

www.jbpub.com

© 2008 Jones and Bartlett Publishers, Inc.

The Coach as Administrator

CHAPTER

25

Planning Practice

Games can be won and lost in practice. Practice provides a coach with an opportunity to prepare for the situations that arise during the game. It also allows a coach to set a tone that personifies the program and presents several teaching moments to prepare his or her student-athletes for life outside the athletic arena.

Some coaches have a detailed practice plan on paper, others may have the detail in their head, and still other coaches do not systematically organize practice. This chapter provides guidelines for an effective practice. The discussion questions ask prospective coaches to consider how to utilize all their players in practice and how practices change as the season progresses. The discussion questions also ask coaches to consider how flexible their practice plans should be and how much conditioning should be incorporated into practice.

The scenarios depict situations where practice plans or practice times may need to be adjusted. A practice exercise asks coaches to create their own practice plan and share it with colleagues.

Warm-Up

This section introduces coaches to two sets of materials important in preparing an effective practice session. The first identifies guidelines for structuring the effective practice session. The second identifies the different components of a practice session, useful for coaches to consider when planning their practice session.

1. Guidelines for an effective practice (Sabock & Sabock, 2005):
    a. Have accomplishable goals and objectives.
    b. Decide how much time should be spent on conditioning, skill development, teaching of plays or strategies, and scouting reports.
    c. Limit instruction to one or two key points.
    d. Maximize space and facilities.
    e. Use time wisely.
    f. Use assistant coaches wisely.
    g. Have partners and scrimmage teams predetermined.
    h. Provide necessary feedback.
    i. Incorporate observational learning or modeling.
    j. Ensure student-athletes perceive that their place on the depth chart may be impacted by their practice performance and work habits.
    k. Incorporate realistic pressure situations.
    l. Adjust for time and intensity as season progresses.
2. Components of a practice session (Robinson, 2004):
    a. Introduction of the practice session

www.jbpub.com

b. Warm-up

c. Review previous learning

d. Learn new skills

e. Game simulations and conditioning

f. Cool down

g. Review

http://health.jbpub.com/book/prepare

Go to the web component of *Preparing the Successful Coach* at http://health.jbpub.com/book/prepare for web exercises and a suggested reading list.

Discussion Questions

1. Critique the above guidelines. With which do you agree? Disagree? Why?

_____

_____

_____

_____

2. a. Sabock and Sabock suggest the first team should never lose in practice. Do you agree? Why or why not?

_____

_____

_____

b. Should the first team practice together as much as possible to ensure the maximum number of repetitions together or should teams be mixed to ensure a more competitive atmosphere?

_____

_____

_____

3. Should the quantity of repetitions for the third and fourth strings be minimized to ensure more repetitions for the first and second strings? Define the balance.

_____

_____

_____

4. What are the benefits and drawbacks of having varsity and junior varsity teams practice together?

_____

_____

_____

5. Should a coach exceed the allotted time devoted to master a new play not going as planned or proceed with practice as planned and come back to the play tomorrow?

_____

_____

_____

6. a. Should the conditioning aspect of practice taper during the season?

_____

_____

b. How much conditioning should be incorporated into today's practice if a team played yesterday and plays tomorrow?

_____

_____

c. How should a coach allow for his or her student-athletes who do not play much during games to stay in shape?

_____

_____

_____

d. How can a coach recognize fatigue, mental or physical, in student-athletes? At what point should a coach cancel a practice to give players a day off?

_____

_____

_____

7. How should coaches balance conditioning with learning in the season's first few practices? How does it depend on the physical condition in which your team reports to the first practice?

_____

_____

_____

_____

8. a. Should a coach ever hold student-athletes past the allotted practice time? Why or why not? If so, for what reason?

_____

_____

b. What if a player, in anticipation that a practice was to conclude at a specific time, has a legitimate conflict and cannot stay?

_____

_____

9. How should a coach balance varying his or her drills with the need for continuous repetition?

_____

_____

_____

_____

10. a. Should a coach ever cancel or stop a practice in the middle of a session because the performance or effort is unacceptable? Why or why not?

_____

_____

_____

b. What are other options available to the coach?

_____

_____

_____

11. Do coaches overemphasize the following?
a. The importance of practice?

_____

_____

_____

b. The importance for flawlessness in practice?

_____

_____

_____

c. The perception teams will play like they practice?

_____

_____

_____

12. How can coaches ensure practice work ethic impacts a player's place on the depth chart?

_____

_____

_____

_____

13. Some players perform in practice but do not perform in games, and vice versa. How should coaches handle these student-athletes?

_____

_____

_____

14. a. Hurley (2006) suggests the development of psychological skills, such as concentration and self-appreciating thoughts, should be included in each practice plan. Do you agree or disagree? Why?

_____

_____

_____

b. What are some specific examples of how these skills can be practiced?

_____

_____

_____

15. Identify some strategies to simulate game pressure during practice. How realistic can a coach make game pressure?

_____

_____

_____

_____

16. a. Identify some strategies to incorporate competition during practice. What is the fine line between emphasizing competition too much or not enough?

_____

_____

_____

b. What should a coach do if better players are "letting up" on weaker players during competitive drills to avoid embarrassing them?

_____

_____

_____

17. a. How is film best incorporated into a practice?

_____

_____

b. Can film make some student-athletes overconfident? Less confident?

_____

_____

c. How should a coach accommodate these student-athletes?

_____

_____

_____

18. How are scouting reports best incorporated into a practice?

_____

_____

_____

_____

Scenarios

1. You give your junior varsity student-athletes next week's practice schedule on Friday. On Monday, you realize you made a mistake announcing Wednesday's practice time. Parents have already adjusted their schedules accordingly to pick up their children. There is no way your team can practice at the time listed on the schedule. What do you do? What are the ramifications with each decision?

_____

_____

_____

_____

2. You receive a phone call indicating that four of your first- and second-string volleyball athletes will miss today's practice because of school bus troubles on a class field trip. You had planned on introducing some new defensive and blocking coverages. Do you still introduce them and expect the four student-athletes to catch up or do you alter your practice plan and wait until tomorrow to introduce the new schemes?

_____

_____

_____

3. Your football team was scheduled to practice this afternoon from 3:00 to 5:00 P.M. A severe storm with lightning has forced you to alter this plan. The volleyball team practices in the gym from 3:00 to 5:00, five of your players have projects in this evening's Science Fair and cannot stay past 6:00, and your gym's dimensions are not conducive to a football practice. Do you practice in the gymnasium after the volleyball team, or do you cancel practice? What are the considerations?

_____

_____

_____

4. A typical practice for your sport consists of various drills, followed by repetitions of offensive and defensive plays you wish to use in future games. It is typical your first- and second-string athletes receive the overwhelming majority of the repetitions during this latter part of practice. Your third-string athletes are often left to watch. Several of your third-string athletes politely approach you after a practice. They do not believe they are being sufficiently included in practice and are concerned they will not have as much experience with the plays if they are ever called to execute them. How do you handle their complaint?

_____

_____

_____

_____

Practice Exercise

1. Prepare a practice plan for a "relatively typical" practice session for your sport. Prepare the plan as if it is one you would actually use. Share your plan with a colleague, ideally one who coaches the same sport. Critique each other's plans for strengths and areas of improvement.

_____

_____

_____

_____

_____

_____

_____

_____

References

Hurley, K. (2006, November). *Healthy head games: Lessons for coaches and athletes.* Paper presented at the Illinois Association for Health, Physical Education, Recreation and Dance State Convention, St. Charles, IL.

Robinson, L. (2004, Spring). Coaches Info Service: Sport Science Information for Coaches. *New coach education—Principles of coaching pack.* Retrieved November 9, 2006 from http://www.coachesinfo.com/category/becoming_a_better_coach/309#organizationof.

Sabock, R.J., & Sabock, M.D. (2005). *Coaching: A realistic perspective* (8th ed.). Lanham, MD: Rowman & Littlefield Publishers.

A team's schedule can have an impact on their season. Schedules are usually made well in advance of the season and may or may not be a coach's responsibility. Schedules are also often made based on predictions of the next season, which may or may not prove to be accurate. Conference schedules may be assigned, but programs do have flexibility in their non-conference games.

This chapter looks at the different things a coach should consider when formulating a schedule or entering a tournament. The discussion questions provide coaches with different considerations, such as the amount of rest needed between contests, pre-season scrimmages, and whether teams should play opponents outside their enrollment classification.

Three different scheduling scenarios are presented. A practice exercise allows coaches to create a month's schedule of games for their sport.

Warm-Up

In this section, coaches are introduced to issues relevant to the complicated task of scheduling. Coaches may have little control over their conference schedule, but how they schedule the non-conference portion of the season may depend on a list of criteria offered for consideration. The components factoring into the decision of which, if any, in-season tournaments to participate in are also provided. Finally, several categories of opponents are identified.

1. Non-conference scheduling depends on the following:
   a. Perceived strength of your team
   b. Perceived strength of your opponents
   c. Perceived strength of conference
   d. Mental toughness and confidence of your team
   e. Playing against teams for which you will compete in the post-season seeding process
   f. Whether every team automatically qualifies for the post-season
   g. Days of rest between contests
   h. Facility availability

2. Components of deciding in which in-season tournaments to participate:
   a. Quality of opponents in the field
   b. Number of opponents in the field already on your schedule, especially other conference foes
   c. Number of guaranteed games
   d. Number of possible games
   e. Likely amount of time between games
   f. Pool play format versus tournament format
   g. Past hospitality by the host, or recommendations from other coaches

h. Travel time and expenses

i. Whether or not you receive a financial guarantee

3. Types of opponents:

a. Automatic win

b. Win if you play well

c. Toss-up

d. Win in an upset

e. Automatic loss

http://health.jbpub.com/book/prepare

Go to the web component of *Preparing the Successful Coach* at http://health.jbpub.com/book/prepare for web exercises and a suggested reading list.

Discussion Questions

1. a. What percentage of non-conference games should a coach schedule against the types of opponents mentioned?

_____

_____

_____

b. What should a coach consider before making this decision?

_____

_____

_____

2. a. Review the components of scheduling non-conference games and tournaments. With which do you most agree? Least agree? Why?

_____

_____

_____

b. What are the advantages and disadvantages of participating in tournaments?

_____

_____

_____

c. What are the advantages and disadvantages of hosting your own in-season tournament?

_____

_____

_____

3. What does a team gain from an automatic loss? An automatic win? Does either make a team better?

_____

_____

_____

_____

4. Can team confidence be inflated or deflated as a result of scheduling? Why or why not? Are there seasons where a coach may purposefully schedule to accomplish such inflation or deflation?

_____

_____

_____

_____

5. What are the advantages and disadvantages, in relation to scheduling, of being a member of a conference or of being an independent?

_____

_____

_____

_____

6. How much rest is needed between contests in specific sports?

_____

_____

_____

_____

7. Should a coach avoid scheduling conflicts with ACT or SAT dates, proms, break periods, important holidays, or other important school events? Why or why not?

_____

_____

_____

_____

8. How far should a team travel for a quality non-conference game? What are the considerations?

_____

_____

_____

9. Should a coach avoid scheduling opponents outside his or her enrollment classification? Why or why not?

_____

_____

_____

10. a. Should a coach enter his or her team into shoot-outs or tournaments that are national in nature? What are the reasons to do so and not to do so?

_____

_____

_____

b. What are the criticisms of such events that have teams compete at a national level?

_____

_____

_____

11. a. What are the advantages and disadvantages of scheduling pre-season scrimmages against an opponent, if allowed by the particular sport governing body?

_____

_____

_____

b. What characteristics of a team should a coach look for when scheduling a scrimmage?

_____

_____

_____

c. What are the advantages and disadvantages of scheduling a formal pre-season intra-squad scrimmage?

_____

_____

_____

d. How many days before the first game should a coach schedule a scrimmage? Why?

_____

_____

_____

Scenarios

1. Your boys' soccer team should be strong next season. You are attempting to schedule tougher opponents to prepare your squad for what you hope is a successful post-season run. A perennial state power will play you, but only on the day before a conference game against an opponent you would classify as a "win if you play well" game. You want to play this state-ranked team but are worried about having to come back and play a challenging conference opponent the next day. The conference game cannot be rescheduled. What do you decide and why?

_____

_____

_____

2. You are in the first season as girls' basketball coach at your school and inherited this season's schedule. Your team is considered below average in your geographical area and is scheduled to compete in a non-conference game against a state power that is 1 hour away. Your team is over-matched against this opponent and loses 74–28, a demoralizing game for your young squad. You inherited a 2-year home-and-home contract with this school, but you do not anticipate a different result next year and would like to break the contract. What are the considerations?

_____

_____

_____

_____

© 2008 Jones and Bartlett Publishers, Inc.   www.jbpub.com

3. You are in the first season as boys' basketball coach at your school. Your team is a charter member of the neighboring community's holiday tournament that has now run for 34 years. Both communities view it as a tradition. Your student-athletes' parents and other fans like it because it is a short commute, and your administration likes it because travel expenses are minimal. You would prefer to give your program a new experience by traveling to a different tournament where they would get the "overnight stay" experience and play teams from other parts of the state. Your athletic director and principal caution you against making such a change from tradition but will not stop you from doing so. They do stipulate that there would be limited budget funds available, meaning you would have to raise some of the monies. What do you do? What are the considerations?

_____

_____

_____

_____

Practice Exercise

1. You are the coach of a sport of your choice (though this exercise may not work great for football). Take any calendar month in which you are in-season. Create an ideal game schedule for your squad, assigning games against conference and non-conference opponents according to the types of opponents described in the background session. You should also space the games and divide home and away contests according to your wishes. Share your schedule with a colleague, discussing the rationale of your plan and asking questions of your colleague.

_____

_____

_____

_____

_____

_____

_____

CHAPTER

27

Overnight Trip and Travel Considerations

Coaches must consider several factors before traveling with their team, especially when deciding to take their team on an overnight trip. They incur many additional duties and responsibilities when they do so.

This chapter provides basic considerations for team travel and discusses the positives and negatives of overnight trips. The discussion questions ask about curfews, room assignments, and releasing players to the parents.

Five scenarios are provided, including a situation where players have been disruptive in the team hotel and where a student-athlete quits the team during an overnight trip. One of the two practice exercises allows coaches to prepare an itinerary for their team's overnight trip, whereas a second one forces coaches to determine how they will make room assignments.

Warm-Up

Here coaches are introduced to the multiple considerations when making travel arrangements for their team, such as the team rules specific to when the team is traveling, including overnight stays. This chapter also discusses coaches' responsibility to school administrators and the bus company when traveling.

1. Considerations for team travel:
   a. Have a detailed itinerary that is communicated to parents, student-athletes, assistant coaches, and administrators.
   b. Have a set policy concerning with whom student-athletes are allowed to travel to and from contests before the first road contest.
   c. Have a roster of the traveling party.
   d. Demand appropriate behavior on the bus and respect for the bus driver.
   e. Establish a rapport with the bus drivers, bus company, and all other entities your team will encounter.
   f. Have emergency contact numbers with you.

http://health.jbpub.com/book/prepare

Go to the web component of *Preparing the Successful Coach* at http://health.jbpub.com/book/prepare for web exercises and a suggested reading list.

Discussion Questions

1. What are the considerations when determining which trips warrant an overnight stay and which trips do not?

_____

_____

_____

2. a. Do the potential benefits/advantages of overnight trips outweigh the potential drawbacks/disadvantages?

_____

_____

_____

b. What are some examples of benefits and drawbacks?

_____

_____

_____

c. Do coaches exaggerate the importance of the "bonding" that can occur on overnight trips? Why or why not?

_____

_____

_____

3. a. How should a coach balance discipline and allowing the players to have some fun during overnight trips?

_____

_____

_____

b. Do student-athletes realize they are representing their school and their community on such excursions? What can coaches do to ensure this realization occurs?

_____

_____

_____

4. a. How should a coach handle curfews and bed checks?

_____

_____

_____

b. Should there be a lights-out curfew, or simply a time student-athletes should be in their room?

_____

_____

_____

c. How should coaches enforce curfews?

_____

_____

_____

d. How should an opposite-gender coach handle bed checks?

_____

_____

_____

5. a. Who should make room assignments, the student-athletes, the coach, or a combination of both?

_____

_____

_____

b. What are the advantages and disadvantages to each answer?

_____

_____

_____

c. Should it depend on whether student-athletes may have to share a bed with a teammate as opposed to simply sharing a room? Why or why not?

_____

_____

_____

d. How should a coach handle a situation where there is one player no one likes nor wants to room with?

_____

_____

_____

6. Some coaches purposefully have their starters room together. The belief is that the starters take getting a good night sleep more seriously and thus will not have players more tempted to stay up late or misbehave distracting them. Do you agree or disagree with this generalization? Why or why not?

_____

_____

_____

7. Should student-athletes be allowed to sleep with their parents? Why or why not? What are the considerations?

_____

_____

_____

8. a. Can student-athletes do their own thing during free time or must everything be done as a team? Why or why not? Does it depend on the presence of parents?

_____

_____

_____

b. Should teams eat together on road trips? Why or why not?

_____

_____

_____

9. Does a coach have the right to check players' bags to ensure they have not brought alcohol or other contraband? Should they?

_____

_____

_____

10. Should consequences for violating team rules concerning alcohol or other vices be increased during road trips?

_____

_____

_____

11. a. What policy should a coach implement concerning student-athletes being able to ride home with parents or other family members instead of the bus?

_____

_____

_____

b. What are the advantages and disadvantages to having a school policy concerning this issue as opposed to allowing each coach to decide for his or her own program?

_____

_____

_____

12. Should coaches instill a dress code in place for their student-athletes when traveling to a contest?

_____

_____

_____

Scenarios

1. The team is going to a fast-food restaurant after the game. Heather's parents are divorced and her father rarely sees her. He wants to take Heather to a separate restaurant where they can spend quality time together. Do you allow Heather to go? Why or why not?

_____

_____

_____

2. You receive a call at 1:30 A.M. from the hotel manager informing you of two complaints from guests concerning noise from a room housing your players. You discover four student-athletes playing cards and being loud. You did not issue a lights-out curfew, so technically no rules have been broken. How do you handle this situation?

_____

_____

_____

3. It is midnight and your assistant coaches are conducting bed checks. They knock on your door at 12:11 A.M. to report two players are not in their rooms or anywhere in the hotel. How do you handle this situation, both presently and later when the student-athletes return safely from sneaking out?

_____

_____

_____

4. You and a player have a disagreement at the team hotel the evening before a game. This student-athlete quits the team and his parents are not available to take him home. How do you handle this student-athlete's lodging, meals, and situation during the remainder of the trip?

_____

_____

_____

5. Your team is playing in a tournament and your game is over at 5:00. The team has eaten dinner and the bus is going to take the team back to the hotel. One group of three players asks you if it is okay to stay with one set of parents to watch the 7:00 game. Another group of players ask if it is okay to go to the movies with a different set of parents. How do you handle this situation?

_____

_____

_____

© 2008 Jones and Bartlett Publishers, Inc.   www.jbpub.com

Practice Exercises

1. You are the head coach of a sport of your choice. Your team will be staying overnight in a hotel during one of your road trips. Assume you are making the room assignments. Also assume you have one player that no one likes. How will you make these assignments? Evaluate how each of the following will factor into your decisions and share your thoughts with a colleague.
   a. Starters rooming together?
   b. Seniority?
   c. Players who are friends rooming together?
   d. Separating potential troublemakers?
   e. Rooming players who do not know each other well so they can get to know each other better?
   f. Rooming the player no one likes with the player most likely to "tough it out"?
   g. Other considerations?

Critique each other's efforts.

_____

_____

_____

_____

_____

_____

_____

2. Complete an itinerary for your team, given the following conditions.
   a. It is a 2-hour bus ride to get to the host site.
   b. Your game on Day 1 is at noon.
   c. Your game on Day 2 is at 10:00 A.M. if you lose Game 1 and at 2:00 if you win.
   d. Approximately half of your team's parents are driving themselves.
   e. Your school's policy stipulates students can only travel with their parents, legal guardians, or on official team transportation.
   f. Your hotel provides a free breakfast.
   g. It is a 10-minute bus ride from the host site to the hotel.
   h. A mall, movie theatre, and other entertainment venues are all within reasonable driving distance in the host community.
   i. There is a separate practice facility teams can reserve for 1-hour blocks of time.

This itinerary should include departure times, meal times, curfews, decisions concerning free time, and anything else relevant to this chapter. Assume you are creating a document you will provide parents and administrators. Share your schedule with a colleague and critique each other's decisions.

_____

_____

_____

_____

_____

_____

EXERCISES 27.0

CHAPTER

28

College Recruitment

Few high school athletes compete on an intercollegiate level. Some student-athletes miss out on opportunities to further their playing career because they are not fully informed. High school coaches often do not appreciate or understand their role in the college recruiting process.

This chapter tries to explain a coach's role in the college recruiting process. The next section offers high school guidelines, defines common recruiting terms, and provides coaches with questions they should encourage their student-athletes to ask colleges.

The discussion questions ask how accommodating and honest a coach should be with his or her collegiate colleagues. The scenarios include a situation where a high school coach becomes aware of a college recruiter's deception. This chapter also includes a scenario specific to college coaches; they are presented with six unique situations during a weekend of recruiting.

This chapter pays special attention to National Collegiate Athletic Association (NCAA) Division III schools, which comprise the majority of NCAA member institutions. It is likely a high school coach will have student-athletes recruited to play at this level, though multiple opportunities to play at colleges representing other NCAA divisions or members of other intercollegiate athletics governing bodies also exist.

This section introduces coaches to information to aid them and their student-athletes in the college recruiting process. First, guidelines are offered to high school coaches on the college recruiting process. Second, several definitions common to the college recruitment process are introduced. Finally, questions are presented that coaches should encourage their student-athletes to ask in the process.

1. Guidelines for the high school coach in the college recruiting process:
   a. Handle reasonable requests for information from college coaches.
   b. Be available for advice to players and parents if needed, but learn your role in the process. Realize your role may be different with each student-athlete.
   c. Be familiar with basic NCAA and other intercollegiate athletic governing bodies and recruiting rules and expect all parties (college coaches and your players) to abide by them.
   d. Be honest in your assessment of a student-athlete's skills, work ethic, and attitude.

2. Common recruiting definitions (National Collegiate Athletic Association, 2006a):
   a. Contact period—authorized athletic department staff may make in-person off-campus recruiting contacts and evaluations.
   b. Dead period—in-person recruiting contacts or evaluations and on- or off-campus official or unofficial visits are not permitted.

c. Evaluation period—authorized athletic department staff may participate in off-campus activities to assess academic qualifications and playing abilities. In-person recruiting contacts are not permitted.

d. Quiet period—in-person recruiting contacts are permissible only on the institution's campus.

3. Questions to encourage your student-athletes to ask of colleges during the recruitment process (National Collegiate Athletic Association, 2006b):

a. What position will I play?

b. What other players will be competing at this position?

c. Who else are you recruiting at this position?

d. How would you describe your coaching style?

e. Who is responsible for my medical expenses should I be injured while competing?

f. What percentage of players graduate?

g. Is summer school available and will my scholarships pay for it?

h. What is the typical day for a student-athlete?

i. When does the head coach's contract end?

j. Will my scholarship be maintained if a new head coach is hired?

k. What are my prospects to have a job?

---

http://health.jbpub.com/book/prepare

Go to the web component of *Preparing the Successful Coach* at http://health.jbpub.com/book/prepare for web exercises and a suggested reading list.

Discussion Questions

1. a. What should the role of the high school coach be in the college recruiting process?

_____

_____

_____

b. Should coaches attempt to steer their student-athletes toward specific colleges or simply be a source of information?

_____

_____

_____

c. Should returning mail and phone inquiries from college coaches be a duty high school coaches are expected to fulfill? What should this duty be during the off-season? The summer?

_____

_____

_____

d. Does the coach's role depend on how much the individual student-athlete and his or her parents need that coach? Why or why not?

_____

_____

_____

2. Do high school coaches feed their ego by where their student-athletes attend college and whether or not they receive an athletic scholarship?

_____

_____

_____

_____

3. a. How difficult is it for high school coaches to truly understand the athletic qualifications to play at a collegiate level in which they are not familiar?

_____

_____

_____

b. How might this be a disadvantage for the student-athletes?

_____

_____

_____

4. a. How accommodating should high school coaches be with their collegiate colleagues?

_____

_____

_____

b. Should practices be open to college coaches?

_____

_____

_____

c. What courtesies should be demanded from college coaches?

_____

_____

_____

d. Describe the ideal relationship between the high school coach and the college coach.

_____

_____

_____

5. Should high school coaches be familiar with NCAA and other intercollegiate athletics' governing bodies recruiting regulations? Why or why not?

_____

_____

_____

6. College recruiters may ask a high school coach about a player's work ethic and attitude. How honest should a coach be when discussing a student-athlete who could improve in these areas? What are the ramifications with being and not being truthful?

_____

_____

_____

7. Should a coach notify his or her athlete in advance if a college coach is definitely going to be at the game? May be at the game? Why or why not?

_____

_____

_____

8. What should a high school coach do if he or she believes a student-athlete's performance is suffering as a direct result of the college recruitment process?

_____

_____

_____

9. What should a high school coach do if he or she is confident college coaches are committing violations while recruiting one of his or her student-athletes?

_____

_____

_____

10. a. Should a high school coach accept perks, such as the opportunity to speak or attend a coach's clinic, from college coaches who are attempting to recruit one of his or her student-athletes? What is the appropriate response to such offers?

_____

_____

_____

b. Sometimes a high school coach may be offered a job on the college coaching staff. What are the ethics involved before deciding to accept or reject such an offer?

_____

_____

_____

Scenarios

1. Your game 90 minutes away from home just ended. It is a school night and you wish to return your student-athletes in a timely fashion. An NCAA Division III college coach who traveled more than 2 hours to attend the game would like some time with you and one of your student-athletes. What should you do?

_____

_____

_____

2. Lisa is the starting point guard for your basketball team. She wants to play point guard in college. School X is recruiting Lisa. Their coach tells you she envisions moving Lisa to the shooting guard position because she believes Lisa's skills are more suited there. You discover School X is not giving Lisa the same message but is instead letting her believe she will be a point guard. What should you do?

_____

_____

_____

_____

Scenarios Specific for the College Coach

1. You are an NCAA Division III college coach attending a shoot-out featuring several high school games. How do you handle the following situations?

a. The first game pits two of your recruits against each other. One is clearly on your "A" list and your college is one of several he is looking to attend. The second is a "B" player who has already committed to your institution and is excited to do so. The game ends and both players see you in the crowd. They are both expecting you to talk with them and will notice if you talk to the other person first. What do you do?

_____

_____

_____

b. The second game features another student-athlete you are heavily recruiting. You have seen this athlete on video tape, hosted him on a campus visit, and have corresponded often with e-mails and phone calls. This is the first time you have seen him play in person. You are taken aback by how much this player gripes to the officials about calls, acts with disrespect toward the coaching staff and teammates, and demonstrates overall poor sportsmanship. The player's father saw you at the game and sat with you; the father's behavior is equally as bad. The culminating point is when the player gets ejected from telling an official a call was bullsh*t and the player's father tells you the official should "f**king lose his certification." How should you handle this situation?

_____

_____

_____

c. You get something to eat after the second game. Another recruit knew you were going to be at the shoot-out and indicated he would come meet you there as he planned on attending the games to watch some friends. The recruit also said he had something you needed to know and it was better if he told you in person. This recruit is a "B" recruit but is the Provost's nephew who would be able to pay full tuition, much to the admissions office's delight. He finds you while you are eating and says, "Coach, nice to see you. My aunt thought it best you hear this from me. I had a scrape with the law last week. My girlfriend is 15 and we were messing around and her parents busted us and had me arrested for statutory rape. Her parents are just being jerks right now, but they'll drop the charges. My coach says the parents are out to punish me because I cut my girlfriend's brother a couple of years ago. But hey, everything is still cool for next year because all this will be over by then; I thought I should tell you." How do you handle this situation?

_____

_____

_____

d. You resume watching games. The next game does not have any players you are currently recruiting but both teams have some good young players for future consideration. NCAA Division III rules prohibit you from talking with sophomores, but after the game a coach from an opposing conference school is doing just that. You do not know what is being said, but it is clearly more than a simple introduction—it is an actual conversation. Granted, the sophomore could be a family member or family friend and you would not know this. What do you do?

_____

_____

e. The games are over and you meet a friend from the area for dinner at a local restaurant. You are simply relaxing with your friend when the older brother/sister of a recruit sees you and invites him/herself to your table. He/she stays and shares a drink with you and your friend. The older brother/sister begins flirting with you. Assume you are single and that you do find this person attractive. What do you do?

_____

_____

f. You return home late and you have a message to call one of your players—no matter how late it is. He was hosting a recruit on an overnight visit. The parents of this recruit explicitly stated they did not want their son around alcohol. You relayed this to your player host and the plan was to go to the movies and then "hang out." You return your player's call and he informs you of a problem. The recruit talked your player into taking him to the parties, where the recruit proceeded to become intoxicated and left the party with a member of the opposite sex. Your host has no idea where the recruit currently is and it is now 2:00 A.M. How do you handle this situation? How do you handle the following individuals: the recruit, the recruit's parents, and your host?

_____

_____

Practice Exercise

1. Review the recent history of student-athletes from your sport and area or conference who have continued their careers at the college level. Also review the recent history of student-athletes from your sport and area or conference who did not. Does any of this history surprise you? In what way? Correlate your analysis as to whether you believe you understand what it takes for student-athletes to play intercollegiately at all the different levels. Share your thoughts with a colleague and discuss each other's responses.

_____

_____

_____

_____

_____

_____

_____

_____

References

National Collegiate Athletic Association. (2006a). *Frequently asked questions on recruiting definitions.* Retrieved October 7, 2006 from http://www.ncaa.org.

National Collegiate Athletic Association. (2006b). *2006–07 Guide for the college-bound student-athlete.* [Brochure]. Indianapolis: Author.

CHAPTER

29

Statistics

Coaches often have the responsibility to keep statistics and records or to delegate this responsibility to a reliable individual. This duty entails more than the simple recording of numbers. It includes how and whether to use the statistics as a coaching staff and how and whether to disseminate statistics to student-athletes and parents.

This chapter looks at what coaches and student-athletes read into statistics. Guidelines concerning keeping statistics are also offered. The discussion questions investigate the ethical dilemmas coaches encounter when keeping stats and ask how much student-athlete's read into statistics. Four scenarios are provided for coaches to consider how to use statistics available to them, whereas a fifth scenario depicts a tough decision concerning a statistician's judgment.

Warm-Up

This section introduces coaches to information relevant to the keeping of statistics. Several software programs now exist for their actual compilation, but the focus of this section is to offer suggestions to coaches on how to handle some of the nuances involving statistics.

1. Guidelines for coaches keeping statistics:
   a. Have command of the official way statistics are to be kept for your sport.
   b. Have a competent person keep the statistics for your team, preferably not a parent or someone else close to one of your players.
   c. Have a systematic approach to updating statistics after games.
   d. Do not allow players to place implicit or explicit pressure on the team's statisticians and official scorers.
   e. Clearly communicate to everyone necessary whether or not you give yourself the right to overrule an official scorer.

http://health.jbpub.com/book/prepare

Go to the web component of *Preparing the Successful Coach* at http://health.jbpub.com/book/prepare for web exercises and a suggested reading list.

Discussion Questions

1. How much do coaches read into statistics? How much should they?

_____

_____

_____

2. a. What are some examples of good play that are not recorded in the box score? Be sport specific.

_____

_____

_____

b. What can coaches do to ensure these efforts receive recognition?

_____

_____

_____

3. What are some examples of good statistics that may not completely reflect good play? Be sport specific.

_____

_____

_____

_____

4. a. How much do student-athletes read into statistics?

_____

_____

_____

b. How can a coach counsel a student-athlete whose confidence is deflated due to his or her stats?

_____

_____

_____

c. What is the fine line a coach must risk between pointing out poor statistics to student-athletes and deflating their confidence?

_____

_____

_____

5. Players can review statistics in the newspaper, but should a coach post them in the locker room or otherwise make them available? Why or why not?

_____

_____

_____

_____

6. How much should a coach rely on statistics or percentage to make strategic decisions? Provide examples of when a coach both should and should not do so.

_____

_____

_____

7. What is the coach's responsibility to ensure the proper way statistics should be kept and/or have working knowledge of the available computer software packages?

_____

_____

_____

8. How can a coach "push the pencil" for their student-athletes? Is this ethical?

_____

_____

_____

9. What is the coach's responsibility to ensure statistics are kept the proper way and to have working knowledge of the available computer software packages?

_____

_____

_____

10. Should coaches keep star players in blowout games to pad their statistics? Why or why not?

_____

_____

_____

Scenarios

1. Mandy is one of your team's softball pitchers. Your records indicate teams are batting .094 against her the first time through the batting order but .308 the second time. How do both a good coach and bad coach use this information?

_____

_____

_____

2. Your basketball team has the ball and a five-point lead with 53 seconds remaining. What factors do you consider before automatically placing your best free throw shooters in the game?

_____

_____

_____

3. Jason is one of your wrestlers. Your assistant coach informs you in all 23 of Jason's matches the athlete who scored the first point has won the competition. Do you tell Jason this? Why or why not?

_____

_____

_____

4. Alice has not played well in her last four tennis matches. Her first-serve percentage has considerably declined since the beginning of the season. You want Alice to be aware of this but also do not want to place extra pressure on her first serve. How should you proceed with this information?

_____

_____

_____

5. Mark has played 55 consecutive errorless games for you at third base dating back to last season. He needs to play four more such games to break the state record. Jackson is your ace pitcher and has an opportunity based on his performance and statistics to earn all-state recognition. There are two on and two out in the bottom of the fourth inning when a tough chance comes to Mark. He does not make a clean play and it is a borderline call as to whether it should be scored a hit or an error. The next batter hits a grand slam and now the decision to score the previous at-bat a hit or an error is the difference between Jackson being charged with four earned runs or zero. Your official scorer is a gentleman in town who has volunteered in this capacity for 22 years. He asks your opinion on the borderline chance. How do you respond?

_____

_____

_____

_____

Practice Exercise

1. Describe the ideal situation as to how statistics will be kept and used for your program. How much personal control over statistics do you want, both during and after the game? How will you use statistics in your game decisions, both in advance preparation and during the game? Share your thoughts with a colleague and discuss each other's assessment.

_____

_____

_____

_____

_____

_____

_____

_____

CHAPTER
30
Game Day and the Off-Season

Coaches have several responsibilities the day or night of a game. Some of these responsibilities are dependent on other support staff. This chapter's discussion questions identify a coach's duties before a contest, discuss the importance of scouting reports, and consider the appropriate time to arrive before a contest.

A scenario is presented that forces a coach to be responsible for additional event management duties at his or her contest. A practice exercise forces a coach to consider all of his or her game-day responsibilities and places him or her in detailed itinerary.

This chapter also reviews the coach's game-day responsibility of crowd control. A coach's demeanor can incite or defuse a crowd. Discussion questions investigate the coach's responsibility and authority concerning the crowd. A scenario asks what a coach should do in a situation where the crowd is abusing one of his or her players.

The coach's season is not over when the final game ends. Coaches have several duties during the off-season. Successful completion of the duties helps coaches to better prepare for the next season. This chapter provides insight into these off-season responsibilities. The discussion questions include how to handle banquets, awards, and new strategies.

Here coaches are introduced to suggestions concerning two separate job responsibilities. The first part offers guidance for a coach on the actual day of a game. The second part offers a coach insight into the multiple responsibilities in the off-season.

1. Coaches' game-day responsibilities:
  a. Game preparation (prepare scouting report, review strategy, prepare assistants, diagram special plays)
  b. Travel (obtain directions, prepare list of emergency phone numbers, confirm bus)
  c. Home event management (ensure the following are ready: press area, support personnel, ticket booth, locker rooms, playing surface)
  d. Personal readiness (mentally and physically)

2. Coaches' off-season responsibilities (Sabock & Sabock, 2005):
  a. Conduct an equipment inventory.
  b. Evaluate the past season.
  c. Provide strength training programs.
  d. Complete the necessary paperwork.
  e. Meet with prospective players and parents.
  f. Organize your staff.

g. Brief the athletic director.

h. Schedule athletic banquets.

---

http://health.jbpub.com/book/prepare

Go to the web component of *Preparing the Successful Coach* at http://health.jbpub.com/book/prepare for web exercises and a suggested reading list.

Discussion Questions

1. a. Are scouting reports as useful as coaches believe? How should coaches use scouting reports?

_____

_____

_____

_____

b. Are scouting reports more for the players or the coaching staff?

_____

_____

_____

c. How are scouting reports, including game film, best used on game day?

_____

_____

_____

_____

2. What game-day responsibilities can be delegated to assistant coaches, managers, and so forth? What should the head coach do?

_____

_____

_____

_____

3. What are the game-day responsibilities of the following constituents?

a. The players?

_____

_____

_____

b. The team manager?

_____

_____

c. The athletic director and school administrators?

_____

_____

_____

d. The custodians?

_____

_____

_____

4. a. How much time before the game should a team arrive to a road contest?

_____

_____

_____

b. What are the ramifications of both being too early and too late for a road contest?

_____

_____

_____

5. a. How much time before the game should a team arrive for a home contest?

_____

_____

_____

b. What are the considerations?

_____

_____

_____

6. a. What do players need to do in preparation for a game? What can the coaching staff do to help them prepare?

_____

_____

_____

b. How much time before the start of the game should the coach have the final team meeting to review strategies and offer final words?

_____

_____

_____

7. a. What should the varsity team do during the junior varsity game of a junior varsity/varsity doubleheader?

_____

_____

_____

b. What are all the considerations?

_____

_____

_____

c. Why might it matter if the doubleheader is at home or on the road?

_____

_____

_____

8. a. What is a coach's responsibility concerning crowd control?

_____

_____

b. Does it depend on the presence of an administrator?

_____

_____

9. Do coaches assume more responsibility with crowd control if the offenders are students as compared with adults?

_____

_____

_____

10. Should a coach have the authority to have people removed from the crowd? Ban people from attending athletic events for inappropriate behavior?

_____

_____

_____

11. a. How can a coach's actions incite a crowd?

_____

_____

b. Is there ever a legitimate reason to do so?

_____

_____

c. What is the appropriate way for a coach to solicit crowd participation from the student body?

_____

_____

12. Can a team's fans impact a program's reputation?

_____

_____

_____

13. What are examples of crowd behavior a coach is both expected to take and should not be expected to take?

_____

_____

_____

14. What are a coach's off-season duties? How much does it depend on his or her contract language?

_____

_____

_____

15. Should a coach be expected to take advantage of professional development opportunities such as clinics or seminars?

_____

_____

_____

16. a. Is the off-season a good time to have student-athletes experiment with new playing strategies? Why or why not?

_____

_____

b. What should be the primary focus for a player's off-season development?

_____

_____

17. a. Should coaches have formal post-season meetings with players? Why or why not?

_____

_____

b. If so, what information should be addressed?

_____

_____

c. If so, how much time should elapse between the end of the season and the meeting?

_____

_____

18. a. Should a team have a post-season party or banquet?

_____

_____

b. Should such banquets be for the entire athletic department, or should each team have their own? What are the advantages of both scenarios?

_____

_____

_____

c. What role should the coach have in preparation? Who else may have roles in the preparation?

_____

_____

d. What should be included in the post-season banquet?

_____

_____

19. a. Post-season awards, who should decide the winners—players, coaches, or a combination of both?

_____

_____

b. What awards should be given? Can there be too many awards? How many is too many?

_____

_____

c. Should the athletic department have a formula for awarding varsity letters or should it be at the coach's discretion?

_____

_____

_____

Scenarios

1. You are the head volleyball coach. Your assistant coach calls you 80 minutes before your home match and says he has to take his son to the emergency room and he will not be able to make this evening's game. Your assistant coach usually greets the opponent when they arrive, ensures the ticket staff has the game programs, and handles all other administrative tasks while you are in the classroom writing the strategies on the board. Your athletic director is undoubtedly still at the cross country meet your school is hosting; you told her earlier in the day everything was covered so she was not planning to arrive until game time. How should you proceed?

_____

_____

_____

2. You are a head coach at your school. Your season did not end well. You suspended two of your starters before the first game of your post-season regional tournament for violating team rules. The parents of these two players were effective in rallying other parents against you and a heated confrontation ensued between you and the parents. Your team, without two starters, played poorly and was upset in the first round of the post-season regional tournament. An unfortunate situation occurred after the game where three seniors aimed their frustrations at you through hurtful remarks. Your program traditionally has a post-season banquet hosted cooperatively by the school and the parents. You currently have no desire to have this banquet and believe it may be best for the program to skip it this season and avoid potential arguments with senior players and their parents. Your athletic director believes this is a situation that you simply have to "tough out." How do you proceed?

_____

_____

_____

3. You are the girls' basketball coach at your school. Your starting post player is overweight. During an away game, student fans of the opposing team harass your player with derogatory comments about her weight. The officials or school administrators do not address this obnoxious behavior. You notice tears welling in your post player's eyes. What should you do?

_____

_____

_____

4. You are the wrestling coach at your school. One of your wrestlers is involved in a physical match. His father becomes out of control after what he perceived to be a cheap shot by his son's opponent. He is screaming at the opponent, threatening to kick his butt after the match. He subsequently becomes verbally abusive with an administrator attempting to calm him down. What should you do, both during and after the match? What should you do if the fan was the opponent's father?

_____

_____

_____

Practice Exercise

1. Prepare a detailed itinerary for when your team has a home contest. This should include identification of all your responsibilities, including your personal obligations, and a time line of when these responsibilities should occur. Share your schedule with a colleague, who preferably coaches the same sport, and critique each other's efforts.

_____

_____

_____

_____

_____

_____

_____

Reference

Sabock, R.J., & Sabock, M.D. (2005). *Coaching: A realistic perspective* (8th ed.). Lanham, MD: Rowman & Littlefield Publishers.

EXERCISE 30.0

Coaching Issues

CHAPTER
31
Legal Issues

Coaches today are employed in one of America's most litigious times. They are also involved in an arena home to more lawsuits than any other component of the educational system.

This chapter identifies multiple areas where coaches need to have a working knowledge of the law, including how to both protect their own rights and the rights of their student-athletes. The chapter provides background information on the areas coaches may have legal responsibility to their student-athletes and examples of coaching situations decided in the courts. Also, important federal legislation is also identified and briefly defined.

The chapter includes discussion questions on the different areas of liability. One such multi-part question asks the reader to identify the coach's liability in a myriad of situations. Another question asks a coach to consider the due process he or she is owed if reprimanded, suspended, or terminated. Three scenarios are presented, two concerning federal legislation and one on a coach's responsibility to a student-athlete who has quit the team. A practice exercise asks coaches to create an emergency plan.

Readers should be aware there are multiple laws and cases that could have been selected and this chapter provides only some of the requisite information.

Warm-Up

Here coaches are introduced to important legal information, including the legal areas of sport and areas of liability for coaches; a brief synopsis on important applicable federal legislation such as Title IX of the Educational Amendment of 1972, The Americans with Disabilities Act, and the Civil Rights Act of 1964; and a short review of examples of coaching issues decided in court cases.

1. Areas of liability for coaches:
   a. Team travel (see Chapter 27)
   b. Supervision of student-athletes at all times when under the coach's care
   c. Unsafe conditions of facilities and equipment
   d. Poor selection of activities
   e. Physical punishment
   f. Instructional techniques

2. Legal areas in sport:
   a. Waivers
   b. Defamation of character
   c. Transportation (see Chapter 27)
   d. Catastrophic injuries
   e. Sports medicine

f. Emergency planning

g. Crowd management

h. Facilities

i. Drug testing

j. Federal legislation

k. Sexual harassment

l. Hazing

m. Employment

n. Due process for coaches and student-athletes

o. Codes of conduct

3. Federal legislation (Appenzeller, 2005):

   a. Title IX of the Educational Amendments of 1972: "No person in the United States shall, on the basis of sex, be excluded from participation in, be denied the benefits of, or be subjected to discrimination under any education program or activity receiving Federal financial assistance."

   i. Three components of the definition:

   1. Claim of discrimination on the basis of sex

   2. An educational program or activity

   3. The educational institution receives federal financial assistance

   b. Americans with Disabilities Act (ADA) of 1990: "A clear and comprehensive federal prohibition of discrimination against persons with disabilities in private sector employment and ensures equal access for persons with disabilities to public services and accommodations."

   i. Components of the ADA:

   1. Prohibits discrimination against otherwise qualified individuals in all programs, including sports.

   2. An individual with a disability can be cut from a team because of insufficient ability but not their disability.

   3. Institutions are expected to make accommodations so that individuals with disabilities can participate.

   ii. Definition of individuals with disabilities:

   1. Individuals with mobility impairments, sensory conditions, mental retardation, and other traditional mental and physical impairments

   2. Individuals with hidden disabilities, including cancer, diabetes, and heart disease

   3. Individuals with a history of having a disability but are no longer disabled

   4. Individuals who do not have a disability but who are treated or perceived by others as having one

   c. Civil Rights Act of 1964: "Persons cannot be discriminated against in employment, including hiring and promotion, on the basis of race, color, sex, religion or national origin."

4. Examples of coaching issues decided in court cases (Lexis Nexis Academic, undated; *Society for the Study of Legal Aspects of Sport and Physical Activity, Incorporated Newsletter,* 2001; Sport and Recreation Law Association, 2004):

   a. Slanderous comments by parents that unfairly lead to the coach's dismissal

   b. A fight between a non-student and an athlete in the locker room before an athletic contest

   c. A football injury allegedly a result of a team playing competition too strong for them

   d. A student-athlete injured during practice on a sports facility not properly inspected for hazards

   e. A student-athlete injured in a game who had not participated in the mandated number of practices

   f. Whether a coach who is terminated had a right to be present at state association meeting where allegations were levied against him or her

   g. A coach requiring a female student-athlete to take a pregnancy test

   h. A student-athlete suspended from a team for speaking out against a coach

http://health.jbpub.com/book/prepare

Go to the web component of *Preparing the Successful Coach* at http://health.jbpub.com/book/prepare for web exercises and a suggested reading list.

Discussion Questions

1. Should a coach ever leave the practice facility without an adult present? What should a coach do in an emergency that requires him or her to leave?

_____

_____

_____

2. a. Who has the primary responsibility, the coaching staff or the school, if a student-athlete is injured in a non-mandatory open gym or captain's practice on school grounds?

_____

_____

_____

b. What precautions should coaches take concerning open gyms and captain's practices?

_____

_____

c. What precautions should coaches take when opening the weight room for student-athletes to lift weights?

_____

_____

_____

3. What duty is owed a player who quits or is kicked off the team during a road contest?

_____

_____

_____

4. a. Who has the greatest duty when deciding to call or delay a game due to inclement weather—the home coach, officials, or the athletic director?

_____

_____

b. What should a coach do who believes the person responsible for making this decision is being negligent and his or her players are subsequently placed in harm's way?

_____

_____

_____

5. Who has the greatest duty to inspect the facilities and equipment—the coach, the custodial staff, or the athletic director? Why? What is the coach's responsibility to inspect athletic facilities?

_____

_____

_____

6. What actions cross the line when a coach is attempting to make the team "tougher"?

_____

_____

_____

7. What is the coach's potential liability in the following situations?
  a. A wrestler gets a staph infection as a direct result of the mats not being properly sanitized?

_____

_____

  b. A coach returns an injured student-athlete into a game against medical advice?

_____

_____

  c. An athlete who had not yet completed the necessary paperwork concerning the pre-participation physical is injured at practice?

_____

_____

  d. A softball player twists her ankle falling into a hole in the outfield chasing a fly ball?

_____

_____

  e. A basketball player is injured upon being fouled hard in practice? The coaching staff had indicated fouls were not going to be called in this particular scrimmage so the team would learn to continue to play through a physical contest.

_____

_____

  f. An opposing baseball player suffers severe facial lacerations after being hit by a pitch? The coach had called for the pitch high and inside to send a message to the batter to back off the plate.

_____

_____

  g. A freshman football player is injured while incorrectly making a tackle? The young man had missed the practice where this instruction was delivered.

_____

_____

_____

h. A swimmer is hurt when a teammate, clowning around, pushes him into the water during an official practice the coach is supervising?

_____

_____

i. A student-athlete is injured in an automobile accident driving himself or herself to a track meet? She received permission to leave early to attend a funeral.

_____

_____

j. A student-athlete is sexually assaulted by a volunteer assistant coach who was not hired according to official procedures? A thorough background check would have discovered this coach had a history of such occurrences.

_____

_____

k. A student-athlete's condition worsens as a direct result that the ambulance was delayed because the assistant coach sent to make the phone call was unaware a "9" had to be dialed to reach an outside line?

_____

_____

l. A tennis player is hurt playing flag football at a practice session? The coach had wanted to break the monotony of practice.

_____

_____

8. a. What are a coach's rights when parents or other community members are slandering or libeling him or her?

_____

b. What should a coach weigh before exercising these rights?

_____

_____

9. a. The due process owed a coach will depend on his or her contract status, employee handbook, and state of residence. What due process should coaches be afforded before being reprimanded or terminated?

_____

_____

b. What due process should head coaches afford their assistant coaches?

_____

_____

_____

© 2008 Jones and Bartlett Publishers, Inc.   www.jbpub.com

10. What are the considerations before a coach elects to do the following with his or her squad?

a. Cut or remove a player from the team who has a disability?

_____

_____

b. Suspend or remove a player for disciplinary actions?

_____

_____

c. Disallow a member of the opposite gender to play on their team?

_____

_____

Scenarios

1. You are the first-year head coach for the girls' basketball program. You meet with the boys' coach to arrange practice times for the upcoming season and are told the boys' varsity team always has the time slot right after school and the girls' have the choice to practice after them or to practice before school. The athletic director affirms this situation. You perceive advantages to being able to practice right after school and correctly believe the girls' team has a legal right to equitable practice times. How do you proceed?

_____

_____

_____

2. You are the swimming coach and practice begins in 3 weeks. Marla, a student with mild cerebral palsy that impacts her psychomotor and cognitive skills, and her parents wish to meet with you. Marla knows how to swim and her parents would like her to join a team both for the exercise and the socialization. They are under no delusions concerning Marla's ability to be one of the top swimmers and compete in the bulk of the meets but are aware the swimming program does not typically have cuts. Marla may need accommodations coming off the blocks to start the race, some instructions both in written and oral form, and other nonintrusive accommodations. How do you approach this meeting?

_____

_____

_____

3. Sean ignores a bunt sign during the first game of a road doubleheader. You bench him, and the two of you have a heated argument in between games. He announces he is quitting the team. You tell him to watch the second game from the bleachers and that he can ride the team bus home. You notice in the fifth inning of the second game that Sean is gone. He has not returned by the time the team is ready to get on the bus for the return trip home. What do you do?

_____

_____

_____

Practice Exercise

1. Create three different emergency plans for when your team is at practice, playing a road contest, and playing a home contest. Include everything relevant in this plan. Share your plan with a colleague and critique each other's efforts.

_____

_____

_____

_____

_____

_____

_____

_____

References

Appenzeller, H. (2005). *Risk management in sport: Issues and strategies* (2nd ed.). Durham, NC: Carolina Academic Press.

Court cases. (2001, Winter). *Society for the Study of Legal Aspects of Sport and Physical Activity, Incorporated Newsletter, 8*(1), 3–6. Gold & Coulson. News/Cases. Retrieved November 9, 2006 from http://gcjustice.com/legal_news_cases.html.

Lexis Nexis Academic. (n.d.). Retrieved July 29, 2006 from http://www.lexis-nexis.com/universe.

Sport and Recreation Law Association. Sport and recreation law cases of interest. (2004, Fall). *The Sport and Recreation Law Association Newsletter, 11*(3), 5–7.

CHAPTER

32

Student-Athletes Who Violate the Law

No coach relishes the day his or her student-athlete gets into trouble with law enforcement. However, coaches need to be prepared for such situations. This chapter investigates what a coach should do during such an occurrence. The chapter also considers the implications when a coach is the one in trouble with the law.

Background information explores coaches' options when one of their student-athletes has violated the law. The discussion questions ask a coach to contemplate whether an athlete already punished through the legal system should face an additional reprimand from the coach. Coaches are also asked to consider the ramifications when an offense is committed during the off-season, and when a coach truly believes in his or her student-athlete's innocence. Situations involving coaches violating the law are also presented in the discussion questions.

Coaches are provided eight examples of law violations and are asked to consider whether both they and their community would deem them minor or major offenses. Six scenarios are provided, including two where the student-athletes are proclaiming their innocence.

Warm-Up

This chapter differs from Chapter 31 by focusing more on student-athletes who violate the law. A coach's options when a student-athlete violates the law are provided.

1. Coach's options when a student-athlete has violated the law:
   a. Automatically suspend the student-athlete until the matter is resolved, at which point a final decision will be made.
   b. Suspend or otherwise punish the student-athlete for a period of time, but allow their return until the matter is resolved—at which point a final decision will be made.
   c. Allow the student-athlete to play until charges are dropped or he or she is found innocent.
   d. Stick by the student-athlete regardless of the legal system's final outcome.
   e. Allow those of higher authority (athletic director, principal) to make the decision.
   f. Entertain teammate's comments to assist in the decision.

http://health.jbpub.com/book/prepare

Go to the web component of *Preparing the Successful Coach* at http://health.jbpub.com/book/prepare for web exercises and a suggested reading list.

© 2008 Jones and Bartlett Publishers, Inc.   www.jbpub.com

Discussion Questions

1. Critique the coach's options when a student-athlete has violated the law. What are advantages and disadvantages of each?

_____

_____

_____

_____

2. What might constitute an example of a student-athlete violating the law but not necessarily a team rule?

_____

_____

_____

_____

3. a. Should a coach additionally punish a student-athlete already disciplined through the legal system? Why or why not?

_____

_____

_____

b. Does it matter if the offense occurred during the off-season?

_____

_____

_____

4. How should a coach handle a situation where a player is in trouble with the law but the charges or the case is still pending? How might it matter whether or not the student-athlete is proclaiming his or her innocence?

_____

_____

_____

5. a. How should a coach handle a situation when a student-athlete is arrested during the off-season?

_____

_____

b. What is this player's status on the team for the next season?

_____

_____

c. What if the player is convicted or pleads guilty during the off-season?

_____

_____

_____

d. What if the player is someone who has not yet been a member of the program, including transfer students, eighth graders, and individuals who have previously elected not to play on the team?

_____

_____

_____

6. How should coaches handle a situation where they believe it is quite likely their student-athlete committed a crime but charges are dropped or the case is resolved but the record is sealed?

_____

_____

_____

_____

7. a. How should a coach balance standing by his or her player who has allegedly violated the law against demonstrating to the team and the community such allegations reflect poorly on the team?

_____

_____

_____

b. Does the alleged crime matter? Why or why not?

_____

_____

_____

c. Does the identity of the alleged victim matter (a fellow student or teammate, etc.)? Why or why not?

_____

_____

_____

d. Does whether or not the coach believes the player is innocent matter? Why or why not?

_____

_____

_____

8. How much does a coach risk his or her reputation sticking up for student-athletes who violate the law? What must a coach consider?

_____

_____

_____

9. Should a coach have a rule that covers being charged with a crime, or should such matters be handled on a case-by-case basis?

_____

_____

_____

10. What prevails in determining what are minor and major offenses—the coach's perception or the community's perception?

_____

_____

_____

_____

11. How might the following offenses likely be classified? How should a coach proceed in each instance?

a. A student-athlete gets in a fight and is charged with battery?

_____

_____

_____

b. A student-athlete receives a curfew violation?

_____

_____

_____

c. A student-athlete is caught shoplifting?

_____

_____

_____

d. A student-athlete is caught stealing street signs?

_____

_____

_____

e. A student-athlete is caught egging houses and soaping car windows on Halloween?

_____

_____

_____

f. A student-athlete is charged with vehicular manslaughter after his or her reckless driving severely injures someone?

_____

_____

_____

g. A student-athlete is caught with illegal drugs in his or her possession?

_____

_____

_____

h. A student-athlete is charged with statutory rape for having sex with his or her underage boyfriend or girlfriend?

_____

_____

_____

12. a. What must be considered before disciplining a coach who has allegedly violated the law? What prevails in determining a major or minor offense—the coach, the school administration, or the community?

_____

_____

_____

    b. How might the following offenses be classified?
        i. A coach receives a DUI?

_____

_____

        ii. A coach is charged with domestic violence?

_____

_____

        iii. A coach is caught with illegal drugs in his or her possession?

_____

_____

        iv. A coach is arrested for unlawful use of a firearm?

_____

_____

        v. A coach is charged with resisting arrest?

_____

_____

    c. How might a coach's contract, or a school's commitment to due process, impact the decision to discipline a coach who has violated the law?

_____

_____

    d. What say should a head coach have in disciplining an assistant coach?

_____

_____

13. How can a coach who has violated the law earn back the trust and respect of the community? Can they? What does it depend on?

_____

_____

_____

Scenarios

1. One of your student-athletes was arrested and charged with assault and battery for allegedly hitting his girlfriend. He proclaims his innocence and the matter will be settled in court. What is this athlete's status on your team until the matter is resolved?

_____

_____

_____

_____

2. Two of your volleyball players inform you they were arrested for vandalism and disorderly conduct last weekend. How do you handle this situation?

_____

_____

_____

_____

3. You are the cheerleading coach at your school. One of your sophomore cheerleaders worked at a local retail store where she was arrested and charged with identity theft and robbery. She allegedly was stealing and later using customers' credit card numbers. She has pled innocent and the legal system will not resolve this matter until after fall cheerleading tryouts. What do you tell this student-athlete concerning her status on the team?

_____

_____

_____

_____

4. You are the golf coach at a school that does not have an athletic code of conduct. Your team rules stipulate a one-match suspension for violating the team's alcohol policy. There is also a separate rule that warrants a minimum one-match suspension for student-athletes who are arrested, regardless of the charges and whether they are eventually dropped. Three of your golfers were drinking alcohol at a party last Saturday night when the police arrived and arrested all the underage drinkers. You are talking with some of your coaching colleagues in the lounge Monday morning. You believe the golfer's actions warrant a two-match suspension, one for drinking and one for getting arrested. Some of your colleagues disagree, stating it should be a one-match suspension because otherwise they are being punished twice for the same mistake. What do you think?

_____

_____

_____

5. Tammy, who will be a junior, is transferring to your school and plans on trying out for the softball team. She approaches you before the season and confesses that she was kicked off the team at her former high school due to some scrapes with the law; she has been arrested both for shoplifting and for possession of a controlled substance. She informs you those days are behind her and she is welcoming a fresh start. What do you do with this information?

_____

_____

_____

© 2008 Jones and Bartlett Publishers, Inc.   www.jbpub.com

6. Your sport is in-season. One of your assistant coaches contacts you on a Sunday. He received a DUI last night and was subsequently arrested when he was involved in a confrontation with the ticketing officer. His spouse, also intoxicated, and young children were in the car at the time of this incident. What is your assistant coach's status for Monday's practice and beyond?

_____

_____

_____

_____

Practice Exercise

1. What is your continuum of law violations as it pertains to how student-athletes will be disciplined? Identify examples or definitions of a minimum of three categories (minor, sub-major and major, for example), and a range of punishment if left to your discretion. Share your thoughts with a colleague and discuss each other's assessment.

_____

_____

_____

_____

_____

_____

_____

_____

Recent incidents have brought hazing into the national spotlight. The Josephson Institute of Ethics (Sharma 2004) cited a study indicating approximately one-fourth of high school athletes state "degrading hazing or initiation rituals" are common occurrences. Hazing occurs in a variety of forms and for several different reasons, and both its victims and offenders represent all genders, races, and sports. This chapter outlines a coach's responsibility to recognize and prevent such nonsense.

This chapter also provides three definitions of hazing, recommendations to prevent it, and components of an effective anti-hazing policy. The discussion questions ask a coach to consider how they will effectively communicate and enforce his or her hazing policies.

Four scenarios are presented. These scenarios depict allegations of past and future hazing incidents. A practice exercise allows a coach an opportunity to create an anti-hazing policy.

Warm-Up

This section introduces coaches to three separate definitions and three separate categories of hazing. Research is also cited offering reasons why hazing is so prevalent. Recommendations to prevent hazing and the components of an athletic anti-hazing policy are offered.

1. Definitions of hazing:
   a. "To intimidate by physical punishment, to harass, to try to embarrass or to subject to treatment intended to put in ridiculous position" (Sussberg, 2003).
   b. "Any activity expected of someone joining a group (or to maintain full status in a group) that humiliates, degrades or risks emotional and/or physical harm, regardless of the person's willingness to participate."
      i. Subtle hazing—deception, silence periods with implied threats for violation, deprivation of privileges, etc.
      ii. Harassment hazing—verbal abuse, threats, wearing humiliating attire, stunts or skits, etc.
      iii. Violent hazing—coerced alcohol or drug consumption, beating or paddling, branding, bondage, etc. (*Hazing defined*, n.d.).
   c. "Any act whether physical, mental, emotional, or psychological, which subjects another person, voluntarily or involuntarily, to anything that may abuse, mistreat, degrade, humiliate, harass, or intimidate that person, or which may in any fashion compromise the inherent dignity of the person" (University of Vermont, n.d.).
2. Categories of hazing based on the sex and violence agenda (Lensky, 2004):
   a. Sexual degradation of men
      i. Forced to dress as a woman
      ii. Forced to purchase feminine hygiene products
      iii. Forced to shave testicles

b. Sexual assault
  i. Forced to have sex
  ii. Forced to participate in gang rape
  iii. Forced to endure sexual assault
c. Physical humiliation with sexual overtones
  i. Forced to consume urine or feces
  ii. Forced to be a servant to veteran players
  iii. Forced to self-injure or self-mutilate

3. Reasons why hazing is prevalent among athletes:
  a. Athletes' identities are tied to their sport and being a member of a team; they will endure humiliation and pain to protect this.
  b. Coaches often turn a blind eye.

4. Conditions to help prevent hazing (Hill, 2001):
  a. Set and communicate clear expectations against the practice.
  b. Ensure captains are on board.
  c. Provide alternate team-building experiences.

5. Recommendations to prevent hazing (Hoover & Pollard, 2000):
  a. Organize community members to discuss hazing and adopt written policies and anti-hazing laws.
  b. Educate administrators, students, and group leaders on the consequences of hazing.
  c. Provide information about the loss of civility and the loss of life that accompanies hazing.
  d. Discuss in detail what is hazing and what is not hazing.
  e. Establish a record of taking strong disciplinary action in hazing cases.
  f. Immediately notify families and law enforcement of suspected hazing.
  g. Take hazing seriously.

6. Components of an athletic anti-hazing policy (Crow & Phillips, 2004):
  a. Hazing must be clearly defined to coaches, administrators, athletes, and trainers.
  b. Alternative team-building strategies should be implemented.
  c. Coaches, administrators, athletes, and trainers must be trained to recognize hazing.
  d. Athletes' off-field behavior must be included in a coach's evaluation.

---

http://health.jbpub.com/book/prepare

Go to the web component of *Preparing the Successful Coach* at http://health.jbpub.com/book/prepare for web exercises and a suggested reading list.

Discussion Questions

1. Critique the definitions of hazing provided above. What constitutes hazing under these definitions? What does not?

_____

_____

_____

_____

2. a. Describe the fine line between hazing and "good clean fun." Is there one?

_____

_____

_____

b. Is having the freshmen carry the equipment a form of hazing? Why or why not?

_____

_____

_____

c. What other ways may coaches engage in hazing under the definitions provided?

_____

_____

_____

3. a. What is the coach's role to ensure hazing does not occur? How proactive should he or she be in stopping it?

_____

_____

_____

b. Should an anti-hazing message be specifically and formally addressed at the beginning of the season?

_____

_____

_____

c. How should the message be communicated to parents?

_____

_____

_____

4. a. What is a coach's responsibility when a player comes to him or her and reports past hazing incidents? Incidents planned for the future?

_____

_____

_____

_____

b. When should the athletic director become involved?

_____

_____

_____

c. Do you agree with Hoover and Pollard that the local authorities should become involved? Why or why not?

_____

_____

_____

5. a. Crow and Phillips suggest athletes' off-field behavior, including hazing, must be included in a coach's evaluation. Do you agree or disagree as it pertains to hazing?

_____

_____

_____

b. How should a coach be held accountable for his or her team's hazing incidents?

_____

_____

c. Critique the remainder of Crow and Phillips' anti-hazing policy.

_____

_____

6. How can a coach counter the following arguments?
   a. That hazing improves team cohesion?

_____

_____

   b. That hazing is no big deal?

_____

_____

   c. That hazing is part of being a team?

_____

_____

   d. That individuals who refuse to participate in hazing activities are not worthy teammates?

_____

_____

7. What are truly effective ways to improve team cohesion?

_____

_____

_____

Scenarios

1. Your girls' soccer team has a tradition that precedes your arrival. Freshmen players take turns standing on a chair in the locker room and singing the school song in front of the team after the third day of practice. You are not comfortable with this but have been unwilling to make an issue of it. What should you do?

_____

_____

_____

2. The parents of two of your athletes contact you with the following allegation: freshmen players were asked to slide through a pool of urine. What should you do?

_____

_____

_____

3. The parents of three of your athletes contact you with the following allegation: selected players were asked to strip naked and simulate sexual acts. The parents also allege one of your assistant coaches knew this was occurring but thought it harmless. What should you do?

_____

_____

_____

4. You coach a spring sport at your school, which endured a lot of negative publicity when one of the fall sports had a hazing scandal. Underclassmen were subjected to removing their clothing, simulating sex acts, and physical punishment. Two of the team leaders that coordinated the efforts played on your team last year. These two student-athletes and their parents have gone on record with their belief that the incident was "blown out of proportion," "in good fun," and "was just part of being on a team." The school administration removed these two athletes from their fall squad, but they are eligible to play on your team in the spring. How do you approach this situation? These players?

_____

_____

_____

_____

Practice Exercise

1. Create an anti-hazing policy for your team. This should include a definition of hazing, punishment for offenders, reporting procedures, and how the policy will be disseminated and enforced. Share your policy with a colleague and critique each other's efforts.

_____

_____

_____

_____

_____

_____

_____

References

Crow, R. B., & Phillips, D. R. (2004). What the law says. In J. Johnson & M. Holman (Eds.). *Making the team: Inside the world of sport initiations and hazing* (pp. 19–31). Toronto: Canadian Scholars' Press Inc.

Hazing defined. Retrieved November 9, 2006 at http://www.stophazing.org/ definition.html.

Hill, D. (2001). Clearing the haze. *Athletic Management, 13*(6), 31–38.

Hoover, N.C., & Pollard, N.J. (2000). *Initiation rites in American high schools: A national survey.* Retrieved November 9, 2006 May 2, 2007 from Alfred University website: http://www.alfred.edu/hs%5Fhazing/.

Lensky, H.J. (2004). Categories of hazing based on the sex and violence agenda: What's sex got to do with it? In J. Johnson & M. Holman (Eds.). *Making the team: Inside the world of sport initiations and hazing* (pp. 83–96). Toronto: Canadian Scholars' Press Inc.

Sharma, R. (2004). *New survey shows high school sports filled with cheating, improper gamesmanship and confusion about sportsmanship.* Retrieved September 17, 2004 from http://www.charactercounts.org/sports/survey/2004.

Sussberg, J. (2003). Shattered dreams: Hazing in college athletics. *Cardozo Law Review, 24*(3), 1421–1491.

University of Vermont policy: Hazing. (n.d.). Retrieved July 31, 2006 from http://www.uvm.edu/%7euvmppg/ppg/student/hazing.html.

EXERCISE 33.0

CHAPTER

34

Classism and Racism

Coaches work in communities of mixed races and socioeconomic classes. Coaches subsequently have to confront the biases of the community, the school system, their players, and themselves. May (2006) argues sports do not necessarily provide the great opportunity for positive interracial experiences as is sometimes portrayed. He also indicates sports are often a place where society's attitudes and stereotypes toward race are manifested.

This chapter investigates the racial and socioeconomic biases athletes, coaches, and fans often hold in sports. The chapter also investigates how socioeconomic class is becoming a more pervasive issue in high school sports. Brady and Sylwester (2004) report the most affluent 25 percent of high schools in each state win state championships at more than twice the rate of those in the bottom quarter.

The section below provides coaches with strategies on how to handle such biases. The discussion questions look at how a coach may get indoctrinated into the community's bias and what a good coach does to make sure racism and classism are not components of his or her program. The discussion questions also critique whether summer camps are a "de facto" form of classism.

Two scenarios are presented. The first situation involves the selection of a black athlete in a predominantly white community. The second involves a student-athlete who cannot afford certain luxuries the team has voted to purchase.

In this section, coaches are introduced to information pertaining to both classism and racism. General data on black athlete participation numbers are provided. Also provided are advantages more affluent high schools have in sports. Strategies to confront both classism and racism are also included.

1. Data on black athletes (Wuest & Bucher, 2006):
   a. Over-represented in football and basketball
   b. Under-represented in volleyball, swimming, gymnastics, soccer, golf, and tennis

2. Strategies to confront classism and racism:
   a. Select the best players, regardless of race or socioeconomic class.
   b. Disallow any racist or classist talk and have policies established for offenders.
   c. Be mindful of the costs "extras" (warm-ups, a second pair of shoes) impose on families.
   d. Respect the fact some student-athletes *need* to work in the summer and make reasonable concessions with your team's summer obligations.

3. Advantages in sports to the more affluent high schools (Brady & Sylwester, 2004):
   a. Better facilities in which to practice and compete
   b. Bigger budgets allow for more amenities to attract student-athletes

c. Bigger budgets allow for higher salaries of quality coaches

d. Wealthier families can afford private instruction and incur the expenses of summer camps and summer travel teams

---

http://health.jbpub.com/book/prepare

Go to the web component of *Preparing the Successful Coach* at http://health.jbpub.com/book/prepare for web exercises and a suggested reading list.

Discussion Questions

1. a. Are black athletes stereotyped to play certain positions in some sports? What are some examples?

_____

_____

_____

b. Why and how do some coaches continue to perpetuate these stereotypes?

_____

_____

_____

2. Are second-tier black student-athletes less likely to make the team in predominantly white communities? Vice versa?

_____

_____

_____

_____

3. What is a coach's role in confronting racism? Does a coach have an obligation to educate student-athletes about racism?

_____

_____

_____

_____

4. a. Do coaches have to fear being labeled racist if they cut a member of a minority racial group from the squad?

_____

_____

_____

b. What other decisions do coaches have to make where claims of racism can surface?

_____

_____

_____

5. a. How should coaches handle situations where their student-athletes use racist comments as part of "trash-talking"? An opponent's student-athletes?

_____

_____

_____

b. Should a coach have an established policy covering such situations or should punishment be rendered on a case-by-case basis? Why?

_____

_____

_____

6. a. How is classism rooted in high school athletics? Is it rooted in the general high school structure? Is it better or worse in smaller communities?

_____

_____

_____

b. Do certain sports attract members of upper classes? Which ones?

_____

_____

_____

7. a. Smith (2006) indicates socioeconomic inequities of communities and high schools are leading to competitive inequities. Would your experiences support this?

_____

_____

_____

b. Critique the list of advantages more affluent high schools have provided in the background. Would you agree the items listed can lead to competitive inequity? Why or why not?

_____

_____

_____

8. a. The Minnesota State High School League (Smith, 2006) became the first high school state association to implement a formula that allows schools with high percentages of students participating in free or reduced lunch programs to be eligible to be placed into a lower enrollment classification, due to the socioeconomic inequities as described in this chapter. Critique this decision.

_____

_____

_____

b. What else can high school coaches and athletic administrators do to solve the growing imbalance between the more affluent and less affluent?

_____

_____

_____

c. What moral obligation do coaches and administrators have to solve the problem?

_____

_____

_____

9. How may members of the following socioeconomic classes of individuals receive preferential treatment?
a. The student-athlete with a rough family background?

_____

_____

_____

b. The student-athlete with a privileged background?

_____

_____

_____

10. a. How should a coach consider the total cost to families when deciding how many summer team camps to enter and where they are located?

_____

_____

_____

b. Is the summer camp structure a form of classism in that student-athletes who can afford to participate receive greater opportunities to improve their skills than those who cannot afford to participate?

_____

_____

_____

11. How should coaches expect student-athletes to balance work and athletics in the summer?

_____

_____

_____

12. a. How might requiring student-athletes to pay for warm-ups or other "extras" be a form of classism?

_____

_____

_____

b. Should a coach allow players to wear warm-ups before a contest if not everyone on the team elects to purchase one? Why or why not?

_____

_____

_____

Scenarios

1. You are the first African-American coach in your predominantly white community. You are finalizing the varsity roster. Antwoin has the talent worthy of a roster slot, but his eligibility has been consistently borderline barely eligible academically and he has had a few scrapes with the law. Antwoin is an African-American. You believe he can strive in the controlled environment your program can offer and want to take a chance on him. You realize, however, selecting Antwoin and thus cutting a "clean-cut" white player has the potential to backfire. Specifically, if Antwoin should fail it makes it that much harder on the next black player in your program. What do you do?

_____

_____

_____

_____

2. Jill is a junior on your softball team. She lives with her mother and two younger sisters in public housing, and money is tight in the family. The captains decided, before the season, the team should all wear the same spikes this year and have the same bags. The team picked out the shoes and the bags and each player and/or family was to contribute $100—the booster club and the softball budget could pay the rest. Jill approaches you that $100 is too great a hardship for her mother and she believes she can get another year out of her equipment from last season. She does not want to be the one player who isn't "part of the group." How do you approach this situation?

_____

_____

_____

_____

Practice Exercise

1. Assess both your life experiences and stereotypes you hold as it pertains to both racism and classism. Have your experiences, attitudes, or stereotypes impacted the decisions you have made as a coach? Share your thoughts with a trustworthy colleague and discuss each other's responses.

_____

_____

_____

_____

_____

_____

_____

References

Brady, E., & Sylwester, M.J. (2004, June 17). High schools in the money also are rich in sports titles. *USA Today*, pp. 1A, 4A.

May, R. (2006, October). Race, sport and the African American athlete experience. In *Building global understanding of race and sport: Where do we go from here?* 2006 Race and Sport Symposium, Iowa City, IA.

Smith, L. (2006). Uneven ground. *Athletic Management.* 18(6): 30–36.

Wuest, D.A., & Bucher, C.A. (2006). *Foundations of physical education, exercise science and sport* (15th ed.). Boston: McGraw-Hill.

© 2008 Jones and Bartlett Publishers, Inc.   www.jbpub.com

EXERCISE 34.0

CHAPTER

35
Religious Issues

Coaches in public school settings may be surprised to see religion as a chapter. However, coaches often have to deal with religious issues involving their student-athletes, communities, or themselves.

This chapter establishes guidelines for coaches when approaching situations involving religion and provides reasons athletes may invoke religion or sport into their athletic lives. The discussion questions involve student-athletes who have conflicts between religious practices and beliefs with athletic practices and contests. The discussion questions also ask what crosses the line in a coach's or student-athlete's religious preaching. The four scenarios provide concrete examples for coaches to contemplate, and a practice exercise asks coaches to record a statement of their beliefs on the subject matter.

Warm-Up

This section introduces coaches to information to help them prepare for the myriad of issues surrounding religion that can make their way into the coaching profession. This can happen regardless of whether a coach is employed by a public or private school. The first part includes guidelines for coaches when approaching situations involving religion, whereas the second part provides reasons student-athletes invoke religion or prayer into sport.

1. Guidelines for coaches when approaching situations involving religion:
   a. Be respectful of those players and assistant coaches who practice religion and those who do not.
   b. Be consistent when dealing with absences resulting from student-athletes who are from different faith traditions.
   c. Understand the need to delineate a separation between your faith and spirituality, or lack thereof, and your coaching responsibilities.
   d. Religious holidays are already on the calendar, but service times may not be announced readily in advance. Establish a policy on the expected communication between the coach and the student-athlete concerning important religious dates that may involve absences.

2. Reasons athletes invoke religion or prayer into sport (Watson & Czech, 2005):
   a. Prayer is used as a coping mechanism to alleviate stress.
   b. Religion and prayer help provide special meaning to sport.
   c. An athlete's religious beliefs are closely linked to his or her motivation.
   d. Religion and prayer place an athlete's sporting life into perspective.

http://health.jbpub.com/book/prepare

Go to the web component of *Preparing the Successful Coach* at http://health.jbpub.com/book/prepare for web exercises and a suggested reading list.

Discussion Questions

1. a. Coaches may have student-athletes who are unable to play on certain days, including Saturdays, for religious reasons. How much should a coach attempt to work around such conflicts?

b. Should coaches exclude religious absences if they have a penalty for missing games? Must they by law?

c. How should a coach handle weddings, bar mitzvahs, confirmations, funerals, or other important religious events in one's life? Is it realistic for a coach to expect families to plan such events around the team's schedule? Why or why not?

d. Should a coach limit which family member's weddings and/or funerals a player can attend and still receive an unexcused absence (e.g., a player can miss for a brother but not for a cousin)?

e. What form of communication should coaches expect from the student-athlete concerning these events?

2. a. Should a team practice on Sundays? Why or why not?

b. Should a coach alter his or her practice schedules or allow student-athletes to leave on Wednesday evenings, a traditional night of worship for several denominations?

c. How about other traditional religious holidays?

_____

_____

3. Should practice be canceled if a coach must miss practice for religious reasons, or should the assistant coaches run it? What messages are being sent either way?

_____

_____

_____

4. What responsibility does a coach have when a player seeks advice from him or her concerning a subject that may be antithetical to his or her religious beliefs (abortion, birth control, homosexual behavior)?

_____

_____

_____

5. When does a coach cross a line in making student-athletes aware of his or her faith?

_____

_____

_____

_____

6. When do student-athletes cross the line in making teammates aware of their faith? What is a coach's responsibility when the line has been crossed?

_____

_____

_____

7. Do coaches face pressure, implicit or explicit, to attend a church in the community?

_____

_____

_____

8. Some athletes are superstitious. Superstition is antithetical to several religions. What responsibility does a coach have to curtail student-athletes' superstitious practices?

_____

_____

_____

© 2008 Jones and Bartlett Publishers, Inc.   www.jbpub.com

Scenarios

1. Several of your student-athletes approach you wishing to begin saying a team prayer before games. How do you respond?

_____

_____

_____

2. You are a boys' soccer coach in a community with a small Jewish population. Yom Kippur, an important day of worship in the Jewish tradition, occurs on the day of an important conference game. Your star mid-fielder is Jewish. His parents have left the decision whether to play in the game to him and he is struggling with the decision. He asks you, who are not Jewish, for advice. How do you counsel this student-athlete?

_____

_____

_____

3. Four of your swimmers come to you before the season and indicate they will miss 3 days of practice in January to attend the annual March for Life rally in Washington, D.C. with their church youth group. They will return the day of a dual meet. What are these swimmers' statuses for the dual meet and why?

_____

_____

_____

4. Five of your student-athletes ask to meet with you. They are alleging that a handful of teammates are asking others whether they are saved. Their allegation continues that any deviation from what the group perceives as the "right" answer results in dismissal, isolation, and a feeling of moral superiority from this group. The five, which include Christians, Muslims, and agnostics, are disconcerted and are asking you ban any talk of religion during bus trips and in the locker room. How do you approach this situation?

_____

_____

Practice Exercises

1. Make a list of all the important people in your life that you would miss work to pay final respects by attending their funeral. Identify the relationships these persons have with you. Share this list with several colleagues. How are your answers different from or similar to your colleagues'?

_____

_____

_____

_____

_____

_____

_____

_____

2. Reflect on this chapter and then write a paragraph or two generalizing your thoughts on how you would handle conflicts that arise between student-athletes, assistant coaches, and yourself and religion. Share this articulation with a colleague and ask each other questions.

_____

_____

_____

_____

_____

_____

_____

_____

_____

Reference

Watson, N.J., & Czech, D.R. (2005, December). The use of prayer in sport: Implications for sport psychology. *Athletic Insight: The Online Journal of Sport Psychology*, 7(4). Available at http://www.athleticinsight.com/Vol7Iss4/PrayerinSports.htm.

CHAPTER

36

Academics

High school student-athletes have varying academic goals, backgrounds, and successes. A coach is asked to monitor the academic progress of these different student-athletes at a minimum of maintaining their eligibility.

Research by Gould, Chung, Smith, and White (2006) suggests a link exists between coaches who have been formally recognized for their ability to develop character in their players and those who take interest in their student-athlete's academic progress. The authors suggest coaches who pay special attention to academics foster academic development.

This chapter looks at multiple issues within the coach's role in the academic arena. It also discusses home-schooled children and their relationship with athletics. Ten tips are provided for coaches surrounding academic issues and information on home-schooled children's eligibility. The discussion questions ask about best practices coaches should use to monitor their student-athlete's academic progress, including the necessity of progress reports. The discussion questions also ask coaches to identify ways to build relationships with their faculty colleagues and to identify and counteract challenges when their student-athletes are enrolled in their classes.

The scenarios provide examples of when the coach's role as teacher and coach may conflict, when a coach may be asked to approach a teacher on behalf of his or her student-athletes, when a coach may be asked to intervene in scheduling classes, and a situation involving a home-schooled athlete. The practice exercise affords coaches an opportunity to create their philosophy statement surrounding academics.

Warm-Up

In this section, coaches are introduced to information to help them prepare for the issues surrounding academics. Several tips are offered for coaches concerning these academic issues, including suggestions for coaches in their academic expectations of their student-athletes and their relationship with the faculty. Also included is information on the hot topic of whether home-schooled students have eligibility as athletes.

1. Tips for coaches concerning academic issues:
   a. Set a tone where academics are important, academic achievement is rewarded, and poor academic achievement is unacceptable.
   b. Become familiar with eligibility requirements for your school, the National Collegiate Athletic Association (NCAA), and other intercollegiate athletics' governing bodies.
   c. Become familiar with your school's graduation requirements.
   d. Become familiar with area colleges' entrance requirements.
   e. Communicate clearly your expectations of academic performance to your student-athletes and their parents.

f. Do not be critical of the faculty in front of your players or their parents.

g. Support the faculty in conflicts with student-athletes involving academics unless there is grave reason not to do so.

h. Maintain a presence, and attempt to build relationships with, the faculty.

i. Realize each student-athlete has different academic goals.

j. Remember players are student-athletes, not athlete-students. Understand the difference!

2. Information concerning home-schooled student-athlete's eligibility (National Collegiate Athletic Association, 2006):

   a. Different school districts have different policies.

   b. Different states have different laws.

   c. Home-schooled student-athletes who aspire to compete at a National Collegiate Athletic Association (NCAA) Division I or II institution must register with the NCAA Initial-Eligibility Clearinghouse. The following information must be provided after registering:

   i. Standardized test score

   ii. Transcript

   iii. Proof of high school graduation

   iv. Evidence home-schooling was conducted within state law

   v. List of texts used through home schooling

---

http://health.jbpub.com/book/prepare

Go to the web component of *Preparing the Successful Coach* at http://health.jbpub.com/book/prepare for web exercises and a suggested reading list.

Discussion Questions

1. Critique the tips for coaches concerning academic issues. With which do you agree and disagree? Why?

_____

_____

_____

_____

2. What role should a coach have concerning his or her student-athletes' academics?

_____

_____

_____

3. **a.** Should a coach send out academic progress forms? Why or why not? What information should be requested?

_____

_____

_____

   b. Should coaches have the faculty complete the progress forms and return them to the coach directly, or can the student-athletes be entrusted to act as the "middle person"?

_____

_____

_____

© 2008 Jones and Bartlett Publishers, Inc. www.jbpub.com

c. What are the advantages and disadvantages to both options?

_____

_____

d. What happens to a student-athlete if one of his or her teachers does not take the time to complete the progress report?

_____

_____

e. Should such forms be sent both during the in-season and off-season? Why or why not?

_____

_____

4. a. Should a coach require a minimum grade point average or a minimum grade in each class for his or her student-athletes to be eligible to play?

_____

_____

b. What is the difference between requiring a minimum grade point average and requiring a minimum grade in each class? What are the potential benefits and pitfalls with both options?

_____

_____

_____

c. What are other examples of eligibility requirements for student-athletes?

_____

_____

5. Should a coach be able to mandate stricter academic requirements than stated in an existing school policy? Why or why not?

_____

_____

_____

6. What are the advantages and disadvantages of states, schools, or governing bodies that have "No pass, no play" rules?

_____

_____

_____

7. a. What are the multiple issues surrounding student-athletes who are home schooled?

_____

_____

_____

b. What are the advantages and disadvantages to the athlete, as it pertains specifically to athletics? What are advantages and disadvantages to the coach?

_____

_____

_____

c. Should a decision to exclude a home-schooled student from participating in athletics be left to the coach, the school, a governing body, or the courts? Why?

_____

_____

_____

d. What would be a valid reason to exclude a home-schooled student? An invalid reason to do so?

_____

_____

_____

8. What are the advantages and disadvantages of mandatory evening study halls for high school student-athletes?

_____

_____

_____

9. a. What role, if any, should a coach have in creating a student-athlete's class schedule?

_____

_____

_____

b. Should a coach encourage student-athletes to take weaker classes during the season? Why or why not?

_____

_____

c. Should coaches encourage student-athletes to drop classes they are failing in order to stay eligible?

_____

_____

_____

10. How may the student-athlete's perception of how serious a coach takes his or her classroom responsibilities impact the message a coach is attempting to send concerning the student-athlete's desired academic performance?

_____

_____

_____

_____

www.jbpub.com

11. Are coaches typically more lenient or strict when their student-athletes are enrolled in their classes? Provide examples of both situations.

_____

_____

_____

_____

12. Describe the ideal relationship between a coach and the faculty. How may it be different dependent on whether or not the coach is a tenured faculty member?

_____

_____

_____

_____

13. a. Should a coach ever ask a faculty colleague to "push the pencil" on a student-athlete's grade? What are the ethical issues surrounding such a request?

_____

_____

_____

b. What is a coach's responsibility when a faculty colleague complains to him or her about a student-athlete's academic performance? A student-athlete's poor behavior in class?

_____

_____

_____

c. What is a coach's responsibility when a faculty colleague praises one of his or her student-athlete's performances in class?

_____

_____

_____

14. What is both a coach's role and responsibility when a faculty colleague accuses one of his or her student-athletes of academic dishonesty?

_____

_____

_____

15. Coaches will have athletes who are aspiring to attend college and others who are not. How do they balance the goals of both these student-athletes when establishing their academic expectations?

_____

_____

_____

_____

16. What are the challenges for coaches who are not teachers in the following areas?
   a. Building relationships with the faculty?

_____

_____

_____

   b. Setting an environment that values academics?

_____

_____

_____

   c. Personally modeling academic achievement and values?

_____

_____

_____

   d. Identify examples of how a coach models academic achievement.

_____

_____

_____

17. How should situations be resolved when an academic field trip will prevent a student-athlete from returning to campus in time for a practice? A game?

_____

_____

_____

_____

Scenarios

1. You are an accounting teacher and head swimming coach at your school. One of your best swimmers is enrolled in one of your classes. You caught her cheating on a test and punished her according to class policy. Would an additional punishment be warranted as a member of the swim team?

_____

_____

_____

2. Your team's great season has resulted in a deep advancement to the post-season, causing excitement in the school and the community. The team will have to miss afternoon classes this Friday to travel to the sectional final some 3 hours away. Five of your players have English last period. The teacher informs these student-athletes of his expectation the student-athletes will submit their 10-page paper, assigned 3 weeks ago and due Friday afternoon, before their departure. Several of your players appeal to you to talk with the instructor and see if he will give them an extension through the weekend; these players have let the excitement of the team's post-season success temporarily distract them from their studies. How do you respond to their plea?

_____

_____

_____

www.jbpub.com

© 2008 Jones and Bartlett Publishers, Inc.

3. Seven of your football players come to you during your third-hour prep period. They have physical education fifth period, but they do not want to exert themselves to be fully rested for tonight's game. The physical education teacher, citing national standards, will not allow the fact they are student-athletes excuse them from their obligation to participate. Your players want you to encourage the physical educator to change her mind. How do you approach this situation?

_____

_____

_____

_____

4. James is your star first baseman and has been a B/B– student during his first 3 years. He has drawn the interest of several colleges and will likely be offered several partial scholarships. You know James wants to attend college to play baseball. You also realize his family is not wealthy and that financial aid will be necessary. James is asking your advice concerning his academic schedule for his senior year. He needs only one more "core" course to graduate, but he wants to take study halls and easy electives the rest of his senior year so he can devote more energy to baseball. You know college admissions and financial aid officers will not take kindly to James blowing off his senior year. How do you advise him?

_____

_____

_____

_____

5. Randi is one of your top golfers. She is dedicated to her sport and demonstrates respect to you as her coach; you have not had any problems with her as an athlete. Randi is taking your accounting class this semester. She has demonstrated disrespectful behavior during class, including text messaging her friends, making inappropriate comments, and otherwise being disruptive. How should you handle this situation, as both her teacher and coach? How would you handle a situation involving the same behaviors if a faculty colleague approached you with this problem?

_____

_____

_____

_____

6. Three of your student-athletes are enrolled in a history class where an opportunity has surfaced for the class to travel to a metropolitan area and tour several museums and historical landmarks. The class will have the opportunity to meet and interact with several historians during the trip. The trip will be an all-day affair, and these student-athletes would not be able to attend practice. The teacher is not mandating the trip but is strongly encouraging it. You have no doubt the trip would benefit your three players, but you had planned on introducing your game plan for the next contest during this practice. How do you approach this situation? What are the considerations?
a. What if this trip interfered with a game?

_____

_____

b. What if the teacher was mandating this trip?

_____

_____

_____

7. Your school district does not have a policy concerning home-schooled children's eligibility in extracurricular activities. Maurice is home schooled and he and his parents introduce themselves and inform you of Maurice's intention to try out for the wrestling team. A handful of parents are disconcerted with this development. They believe Maurice has an unfair advantage because he does not have to endure the "rigors of an average high school day." They want you to disallow Maurice from trying out for the team and are willing to take the matter to the athletic director should you decline. How do you handle this situation?

_____

_____

_____

_____

Practice Exercise

1. Create a philosophy statement concerning your student-athletes' academic achievement. Include any of the components detailed in this chapter you deem necessary. Share your statement with a colleague and critique each other's efforts.

_____

_____

_____

_____

_____

_____

_____

_____

_____

References

Gould, D., Chung, Y., Smith, P., & White, J. (2006, September). Future directions in coaching life skills: Understanding high school coaches' views and needs. *Athletic Insight: The Online Journal of Sport Psychology, 8*(3). Retrieved November 9, 2006 from http://www.athleticinsight.com/Vol8Iss3/CoachingLifeSkills.htm.

National Collegiate Athletic Association. (2006). *Frequently asked questions about home schooling.* Retrieved October 14, 2006 at http://www1.ncaa.org/membership/membership_svcs/eligibility-recruiting/faqs/homeschooling.

CHAPTER
37
Sex and Gender Issues

High school is a time when young women and men are developing their sexual identity. Many are exploring their sexuality through behaviors they are likely not mature enough to handle, though recent findings suggest sexual activity among high school students is declining. An average high school team will likely have student-athletes at all points on the spectrum of sexual experience and behaviors, and a coach may directly or indirectly be called upon for his or her advice.

Student-athletes may be comfortable confiding in their coach concerning such matters, especially in the absence of other adult role models. Coaches may or may not be comfortable participating in such conversations. However, both athletes and coaches may be less comfortable when the coach is of opposite gender than the player.

This chapter explores the issues related to sex and gender, including coaching the opposite gender. Guidelines are provided for meetings between a coach and a player of the opposite gender who has exhibited inappropriate behavior. Definitions and examples of sexual harassment are also provided. Research specific to reasons female athletes quit participating in sports and their perceptions and experiences with both male and female coaches is covered.

The discussion questions focus on how opposite-gender coaches can overcome certain obstacles, what is appropriate behavior in opposite-gender situations, and the role of the coach as an educator and role model in the area of sex. Eleven behaviors are outlined and coaches are asked whether or not these behaviors must be avoided. The scenarios provide situations where future and current coaches can discuss the appropriateness of certain behaviors. Included are occurrences involving a website, inappropriate comments from male and female student-athletes, and alleged misbehavior from assistant coaches.

Warm-Up

This section introduces coaches to several topics pertaining to different sex and gender issues. Guidelines are provided for coaches when meeting with an opposite-gender student-athlete. The definitions and types of sexual harassment are presented. Research is presented on the attitudes of female athletes' experiences with both male and female coaches and the reasons female student-athletes quit sports.

1. Guidelines for meetings between a coach and a player of opposite gender who has acted inappropriately (Alberts, 2003):
   a. A third party should be present or the meeting should be held in a place in full view of others. A desk should separate the player and coach if the meeting must be held in private.
   b. The coach should maintain a professional demeanor and outline specific examples of inappropriate behavior and/or actions.

© 2008 Jones and Bartlett Publishers, Inc.   www.jbpub.com

   c. The coach may need to define the boundaries of a coach–player relationship.

   d. The meeting should be closed on a positive note, but not without the player understanding the ramifications of future similar actions.

2. Types of sexual harassment (Cotton & Wolohan, 2003):

   a. Quid pro quo (this for that). An example is, "I will place you on the team or in the starting line-up if you have sex with me."

   b. Hostile environment. The surroundings or situations in an environment are so unpleasant that the victim's presence makes it difficult to coexist. An example is a player's reaction to a coach who is "looking them over" or who makes inappropriate comments toward sex or specific men or women.

3. Recommendations to ensure maximum safety of student-athletes from coaches who are sexual predators (Wilson, 2006):

   a. Ensure all your assistant coaches or volunteer coaches have undergone background checks; coaches should do it themselves if the administration will not.

   b. Avoid occurrences where coaches are with just one student-athlete alone outside a team function.

   c. Touching student-athletes may occur while coaching them. Establish what is appropriate and inappropriate and create an environment where student-athletes can communicate their discomfort.

4. Results of a study researching attitudes of female athletes' experiences with and perceptions of male and female coaches (Frey, Czech, Kent, & Johnson, 2006):

   a. The female athletes thought their male coaches were better organized than their female counterparts.

   b. The female athletes thought their male coaches were more authoritative than their female counterparts.

   c. The female athletes thought their female coaches had a better ability to relate to them than their male counterparts.

   d. The female athletes thought their female coaches better understood how to deal with situations female athletes encounter than their male counterparts.

   e. The female athletes thought their female coaches were more likely to play favorites than their male counterparts.

   f. The majority of female athletes prefer having male coaches.

5. Results of a study identifying common reasons female student-athletes quit sports (Stewart & Taylor, 2000):

   a. The study, conducted on junior and senior high school athletes in the state of Montana, found the following reasons:

     i. Injury

     ii. Time conflicts

     iii. Issues with the coaching staff

     iv. The experience ceased being fun

   b. The authors concluded female athletes play sports as much for the social interactions as the competitive aspects.

---

http://health.jbpub.com/book/prepare

Go to the web component of *Preparing the Successful Coach* at http://health.jbpub.com/book/prepare for web exercises and a suggested reading list.

Discussion Questions

1. a. Is it best for student-athletes to have a coach of the same gender? Why or why not?

_____

_____

_____

b. What are the definite advantages? Possible disadvantages?

_____

_____

_____

2. a. What obstacles may opposite-gender coaches encounter in their ability to effectively build positive coach–player relationships? Do they have any advantages?

_____

_____

_____

b. How may the answer be different when comparing men who are coaching girls with women who are coaching boys?

_____

_____

_____

3. What obstacles may homosexual coaches coaching the same gender as themselves encounter in their ability to effectively build positive coach–player relationships? Do they have any advantages?

_____

_____

_____

4. a. How should opposite-gender coaches protect themselves at practice or during games?

_____

_____

_____

b. What is appropriate practice attire for players during practice situations? Should players' practice attire be different with opposite-gender coaches?

_____

_____

_____

5. What should coaches do if they suspect a player has a romantic crush on them? If they believe they are developing a crush on a player?

_____

_____

_____

6. How may coaches be expected to be careful in their personal dating and sexual life? Answer the following questions both for the same-gender and opposite-gender coach.

    a. Do coaches lose credibility with their student-athletes and/or parents if they are reputed to frequent the local strip bar?

_____

_____

    b. Do coaches lose credibility with their student-athletes and/or parents if they are reputed to have several one-night stands?

_____

_____

    c. Do coaches lose credibility with their student-athletes and/or parents if they are reputed to be cheating on their significant other?

_____

_____

7. Should a coach do the following, regardless of what gender student-athletes he or she is coaching?

    a. Engage in conversations concerning his or her student-athletes' sex lives?

_____

_____

    b. Make casual remarks about any person's sex appeal?

_____

_____

    c. Make sure overnight romantic guests do not park close to his or her house?

_____

_____

    d. Rent a pornographic video at the local video store?

_____

_____

    e. View pornography in any form?

_____

_____

    f. Have a one-night stand with a person from the community?

_____

_____

g. Have an affair with a married person from the community?

_____

_____

h. Dress in revealing clothing in a public place?

_____

_____

i. Should female coaches ever wear clothing showing cleavage, even if it would largely be considered in good taste? Should a female coach ever wear such an outfit during a game? Why or why not?

_____

_____

_____

j. Date an older sibling or parent of a student-athlete?

_____

_____

k. Have casual sex with an older sibling or parent of a student-athlete?

_____

_____

8. a. What should a coach do when a player comes to him or her with a question concerning the player's sex life? Does it matter if the coach is of the same or opposite gender?

_____

_____

b. Should a coach be expected to "err on the side of caution" and thus promote waiting to have sex or complete abstinence? Why or why not?

_____

_____

9. a. Is a female student-athlete's menstrual cycle a coach's business? Why or why not?

_____

_____

b. Is a female student-athlete's menstrual cycle the athletic trainer's business? Why or why not?

_____

_____

c. What should a coach do when a female player states she is having physical discomfort resulting from her menses?

_____

_____

d. Does the answer depend on whether the coach is male or female? Why or why not?

_____

_____

Scenarios

1. How should a male coach handle the following situation? He is with the team at a restaurant for a post-game meal. An attractive well-endowed woman with a low-cut shirt is at the restaurant. Players are making comments about her chest after she leaves. A player asks the coach what he thinks.

_____

_____

_____

_____

2. How should a female coach handle the following situation? She is with the team in the locker room. One player asks a teammate how she got the carpet burns on her knees (insinuating performing oral sex). The players begin to laugh cautiously as they await the coach's reaction.

_____

_____

_____

_____

3. A student-athlete approaches you concerning his or her life. He or she is a virgin and believes his or her current boyfriend/girlfriend is pressuring him or her into having sex. How should you counsel this student-athlete?

_____

_____

_____

4. Drew has joined your girls' volleyball coaching staff while student teaching at the school. Your captains request a meeting with you 3 weeks into the season. They allege Drew is constantly attempting to look down their shirts or otherwise "check them out." One of your player's brothers attends the same college as Drew and the rumor is that Drew spends a lot of time watching pornographic movies. You do not know if the allegation or the rumor is true, but you are confident your captains are truthful in that the team is uncomfortable around Drew. How do you approach this situation?

_____

_____

_____

5. You are the head coach of a boys' varsity sport. Your junior varsity had a road contest this afternoon and your assistant coach accompanied the team. You receive a telephone call at home from your principal. She has fielded three phone calls from parents complaining the team ate dinner on the way home at a restaurant famous for its waitresses' revealing attire. You inform the principal you did not have advance knowledge of your assistant coach's intent to take the team there.

The principal believes you, but expects you to handle this situation appropriately. What do you do?

_____

_____

_____

_____

6. It has been brought to your attention that four of your student-athletes have posted graphic pictures and descriptions of their past sexual escapades on a website known as a site where friends can stay connected. You do not have a team rule governing such action, but you believe such depictions reflect poorly on your team. How do you handle this situation?

_____

_____

_____

_____

Practice Exercise

1. Identify what you believe would be to your advantage and disadvantage in your ability to coach the opposite gender. Why do you believe this? Share your thoughts with a colleague and discuss each other's responses.

_____

_____

_____

_____

_____

_____

_____

_____

_____

References

Alberts, C.L. (2003). *Coaching issues & dilemmas: Character building through sport participation.* Reston, VA: National Association for Sport and Physical Education.

Cotton, D.J., & Wolohan, J.T. (2003). *Law for recreation and sport managers* (3rd ed.). Dubuque, IA: Kendall/Hunt Publishing Company.

Frey, M., Czech, D.R., Kent, R.G., & Johnson, M. (2006, Fall). An exploration of female athletes' experiences and perceptions of male and female coaches. *The Sport Journal, 9*(4). Retrieved November 9, 2006 from http://www.thesportjournal.org/2006Journal/Vol9-No4/Frey.asp.

Stewart, C., & Taylor, J. (2000). Why female athletes quit: Implications for coach education [Electronic version]. *Physical Educator, 57*(4).

Wilson, K. (2006). *Protection for kids in youth sports: Stopping sexual predators.* Retrieved August 1, 2006 from http://www.momsteam.com/alpha/features/parenting/stopping_sexual_predators2.shtml.

CHAPTER
38
The Summer

The summer has become an increasingly important part of the high school sports season. State high school associations have attempted to curb abuses while simultaneously accommodating coaches' perceived needs.

This chapter reviews the importance of the summer to the team's progression, fair expectations of student-athletes, and the coach's responsibilities. Guidelines are provided for coaches to implement when planning for the summer. The discussion questions ascertain the importance of the summer in evaluating talent and building team chemistry and also determine the attendance requirements for both the student-athlete and the coach in the summer.

The discussion questions also review the potential conflicts that arise with two-sport athletes and vacations. The scenarios depict two such conflicts and include a situation where a star player wants to miss team camps to attend individual camps. A practice exercise asks a coach to prepare for the summer using all of the material presented.

Warm-Up

This section introduces coaches to their summer duties and the issues surrounding those duties. Specific guidelines for coaches to implement when planning for the summer are provided. These include the best way for a coach to communicate his or her summer intentions to all parties and to be mindful of the multiple other aspects of the student-athletes' and staff's lives.

1. Guidelines for coaches to implement when planning for the summer:
   a. Announce the schedule of practices, team camps, and summer leagues as early as possible.
   b. Communicate clearly your expectations of student-athletes' attendance at events.
   c. Be mindful of family vacations, including your own.
   d. Be mindful of student-athletes who participate in multiple sports.
   e. Be mindful of students who have a job to offset family expenses.
   f. Be mindful of the costs families incur with various travel expenses.

http://health.jbpub.com/book/prepare

Go to the web component of *Preparing the Successful Coach* at http://health.jbpub.com/book/prepare for web exercises and a suggested reading list.

Discussion Questions

1. a. What is the fair expectation for a coach to have for his or her student-athletes in the summer?

_____

_____

_____

b. The Illinois High School Association (2006) states "participation in summer programs must be voluntary and in no way be an actual or implied prerequisite for membership on a high school team." Critique this statement, both on its ideology and its ability to be enforced.

_____

_____

_____

2. What is the fair expectation for a coach to have for his or her staff during the summer?

_____

_____

_____

_____

3. a. What are other priorities in student-athletes' lives during the summer?

_____

_____

_____

b. Are any of these legitimate reasons to miss scheduled summer workouts or practices? How should a student-athlete balance his or her sport and other priorities?

_____

_____

_____

c. Critique the guidelines provided above in lieu of the preceding question, specifically the four areas where coaches are encouraged to "be mindful."

_____

_____

_____

d. How should conflicts with other sports be resolved? Should the student-athlete and all applicable coaches sit down to discuss the summer before it begins? What are other considerations?

_____

_____

_____

4. How valuable is the summer in terms of being able to evaluate talent for the next season?

_____

_____

_____

5. How valuable is the summer in terms of being able to build team chemistry? Do coaches over-rate or underestimate the importance of either or both?

_____

_____

_____

_____

6. How much of the summer should a coach be expected to devote to his or her coaching duties? How may it depend on contractual language?

_____

_____

_____

_____

7. Should a coach be expected to run a summer camp? Should the profits belong to the coach or the program?

_____

_____

_____

_____

8. a. Some high school state associations allow coaches to have contact with their student-athletes for a set period of days during the summer. Should a coach maximize this contact? Why or why not?

_____

_____

_____

b. How does the pressure to stay competitive with other programs impact this decision? Does this pressure get overblown? Why or why not?

_____

_____

c. How should a coach balance using this contact time for skill development as opposed to practicing game strategies?

_____

_____

d. How should physical conditioning be included in the summer?

_____

_____

e. What are the positives and negatives with state high school associations allowing coaches to have formal contact with their student-athletes during the summer?

_____

_____

_____

Scenarios

1. a. An athlete who plays both basketball and baseball faces several conflicts when his or her American Legion games interfere with basketball summer league games. How should this be worked out?

_____

_____

b. Should either of the high school coaches have any say in the matter?

_____

_____

c. What if this athlete was a volleyball/basketball player—should the fall sport receive priority in the summer?

_____

_____

2. Your star player wants to attend several prominent individual camps to gain exposure. Several of these are held simultaneously with team camps you wished to enter. How should this be worked out?

_____

_____

_____

3. Your spouse works at the local factory. The plant shuts down for 2 weeks in the summer, the only vacation time your spouse receives all year. The shutdown conflicts with two of the area's best team camps. What do you do? What are the considerations involved?

_____

_____

_____

Practice Exercise

1. You are allowed 30 days to coach your team in the summer. Answer the following questions in a paragraph articulating your preparation, and then share your articulations with a colleague and critique each other's efforts.

a. How many practices do you want to have?

_____

_____

_____

_____

_____

b. Who will you invite to practice?

_____

_____

_____

_____

_____

c. What will be the attendance policy for both your players and your assistant coaches?

_____

_____

_____

_____

_____

d. What are the main things you wish to accomplish?

_____

_____

_____

_____

_____

Reference

Illinois High School Association. (2006, July 1). 2006–07 IHSA handbook: Constitution, by-laws with illustrations, and policies. Retrieved November 13, 2006 from http://www.ihsa.org/org/policy/section3.pdf.

EXERCISE 38.0

Conclusion

CHAPTER
39

Practice Test Questions

1. You are the head coach for a winter sport. What expectations would you place on your student-athletes who are currently playing a fall sport? What restrictions would your place on your student-athletes planning on playing a spring sport? How will you communicate your expectations and restrictions to both your student-athletes and your coaching colleagues?

_____

_____

_____

_____

_____

_____

2. You are the head coach of a high school sport of your choice. How many players do you want on your squad? What will be the predominant characteristics you will look for in your third-string student-athletes? How will you balance a prospective player's attitude, talent, and potential? What will you do with the seniors who may not see much playing time? How will you cut the 10 individuals you need to cut?

_____

_____

_____

_____

3. Everything a coach does sets a precedent. What does this mean? How may the unwillingness to set precedent affect your decisions? Provide examples.

_____

_____

_____

_____

_____

_____

4. Two of your starters were deemed ineligible for the remainder of the season. They violated the school's athletic code of conduct three times, all alcohol violations. The players sued and won an injunction against the school. The court ruled the two cannot be removed from the team without due process. The court does not stipulate they have any right to play, only that they cannot be removed from the roster. Do these two student-athletes play in the next game? Why or why not? What are all of the considerations?

_____

_____

_____

_____

_____

_____

5. You are a first-year head coach of a sport of your choice. The athletic director suggests you have an introductory meeting with the parents. What do you include in this meeting? What do you avoid? What tone do you attempt to set? How will you attempt to contact the parents who are unable to attend the meeting?

_____

_____

_____

_____

_____

_____

6. What must a coach consider before scheduling a game requiring overnight travel? What must a coach consider when preparing for an overnight trip? Include in your answer the following components: whether you would give your players free time, whether all players must do the same thing during free time, curfews and bed checks, and parental involvement.

_____

_____

_____

_____

_____

7. Your female assistant coach and the father of one of your players ask if they can come to your house and talk. They arrive and inform you they are having an affair. Your player's father is still married and your player just recently learned of the affair. You are not happy with this development, but both parties to the affair are consenting adults. How do you handle this situation?

_____

_____

_____

_____

_____

8. Your starting running back was injured 3 weeks ago. This week is your regular season finale and your team has already qualified for the playoffs. You ideally want to give your running back some playing time this week so he can work out the kinks before the playoff game. The team doctor has cleared him to play but the athlete and his parents are insistent on waiting 1 more week to be fully healed for the playoffs. What do you do and why?

_____

_____

_____

_____

9. Your basketball team returns several players next season and there will be a certain level of expectation. Your conference is projected to be weaker next year. You are responsible for your own scheduling. How many games do you schedule (assume 12 non-conference games) for each of the following and why: definite wins, win if you play well, toss-ups, win in an upset, definite losses?

_____

_____

_____

_____

10. Four of your players contact you during the summer concerning next season's schedule. The bishop has just announced the date he is coming to town for confirmation and there is a conflict. These four players have already committed to serve as their siblings' confirmation sponsor. The bishop only comes to a community once every 2 or 3 years and he will not reschedule due to your game. How do you approach this situation?

_____

_____

_____

_____

11. Identify eight adjectives describing a good coach. Write a minimum of one sentence describing how each adjective is relative to the coaching profession.

_____

_____

_____

12. Your last home game of the regular season will decide the conference championship. You have two third-string seniors who have given the program 4 years of hard work. Will you start them? Be sure to play them? How will you or won't you incorporate them into the game? Describe how you will handle this situation.

_____

_____

_____

_____

13. You are the head coach of a sport of your choice. What will you expect/demand from your athletes in the summer? What must you consider before placing such demands?

_____

_____

_____

_____

_____

14. You are a first-year head coach and will have the opportunity to host a camp next summer. Will you make a reasonable effort to schedule your camp around those of other coaches at your school to avoid placing two-sport athletes in a difficult situation? Will junior high students be invited and/or encouraged to attend? How will you handle the campers whose talent level does not make them a realistic prospect for your program?

_____

_____

_____

_____

_____

15. A parent of one of your tennis players pulls to a screeching halt in the parking lots near the courts where today's match is occurring. The parent gets out of the car and screams at his child to get home right now. You have no idea what this is about, but the parent is belligerent and causing a scene. You approach the parent and inform him his child's match is underway. You politely inform him a substitute cannot be entered at this point and he is causing a scene while embarrassing his child. You are loudly told to "Mind your f**king business." How do you approach this situation?

_____

_____

_____

_____

16. You are cleaning in the locker room when you hear two of your student-athletes engaged in a conversation. Your pitcher, who earlier today threw a shutout, is telling a teammate how he illegally concealed and used pine tar on the ball. How do a good coach and a bad coach handle this?

_____

_____

_____

_____

_____

17. You are in the pre-season of your winter sport. Your team is scheduled to practice Friday after school and on Saturday morning. The school's volleyball team successfully advanced to the state tournament on Tuesday evening. Several of your players would like to attend the state volleyball tournament and your athletic director believes you should make "reasonable accommodations" to your practice schedule to allow for your athletes to cheer on their schoolmates. It is a 2-hour drive to the state tournament; the volleyball team plays at 4:00 on Friday and will play at 11:00 A.M. on Saturday if they win. How do you proceed?

_____

_____

_____

_____

_____

18. What are the advantages, disadvantages, and considerations of hiring someone with previous head coaching experience to join your staff as an assistant coach?

_____

_____

_____

19. What are your goals for the pre-game speech? What do you want to emphasize? What final teaching points will you cover? How fired up will you get?

_____

_____

_____

_____

_____

20. You receive a letter that is severely critical of your handling of your team, recent game decisions, and your selections of the starting line-up. The note is simply signed "an anonymous parent." How do you handle this situation?

_____

_____

_____

_____

21. Would you prefer to coach at a high school with only one junior high feeder school or multiple junior highs? What are the advantages and disadvantages to both situations? Explain your answer.

_____

_____

_____

_____

© 2008 Jones and Bartlett Publishers, Inc.   www.jbpub.com

22. Your softball budget provides a dollar allocation for bats. Some of your players prefer buying their own bats, believing they are of higher quality than what the team provides. A recent incident occurred where one of your players did not share her personal bat with another player, saying it was an expensive bat and her teammate should buy her own. You know this teammate's family could never afford such an expensive bat and some teammates, more representative of the team's "have nots," rushed to her defense. How should a coach handle this situation? What are the considerations?

_____

_____

_____

_____

_____

23. One of your players commits a "cheap shot" against a teammate during practice. You immediately eject this player from practice. You do not have a team rule that covers unnecessary rough play or being ejected from a practice. What is this player's status on the team for tomorrow's practice? How do you handle this situation?

_____

_____

_____

_____

_____

24. What does a head coach owe the following constituents upon being ejected from a game for excessive arguing with officials: his or her student-athletes, his or her coaching staff, the opponents, the fans, his or her school administration, and the officials?

_____

_____

_____

_____

_____

25. What have you learned about yourself after reading *Preparing the Successful Coach*? What have you learned about others who may have read the book with you? How has *Preparing the Successful Coach* assisted you to gain a broader perspective of the coaching profession? How has it assisted in the advancement of your coaching philosophy?

_____

_____

_____

_____

_____

Index

Notes

Notes

Notes

Notes

Notes